THEATRE ROYAL STRATFORD EAST PRESENTS

GUTTED

By Rikki Beadle-Blair

First performed at Theatre Royal Stratford East
on Friday 26 April 2013

CAST
(in alphabetical order)

Frankie/Moses	**Ashley Campbell**
Lucy Lockwood	**Jennifer Daley**
Matthew Prospect	**James Farrar**
Mark Prospect	**Frankie Fitzgerald**
Janine Lockwood-Prospect	**Sasha Frost**
Bridie Prospect	**Louise Jameson**
John Prospect	**Gavin McCluskey**
Sunai Suleyman	**Dominique Moore**
Luke Prospect	**Jamie Nichols**

CREATIVE TEAM

Writer/Director/Designer	**Rikki Beadle-Blair**
Lighting Designer	**Michael Nabarro**
Sound Designer	**Theo Holloway**
Assistant Costume Designer/ Wardrobe Manager	**Holly Owst**

Music by **Rikki Beadle-Blair**, performed and produced by **Joni Levinson** and **Rikki Beadle-Blair**
Assistant Directors: **Shante Campbell, Kizzy Kaye, Lynette Linton**
Trainee Directors: **Stephen Lloyd, Debra Baker, Afia Abusham, Justin Donaldson, Enrico Tessarin, Adam Lannon, Simon Schultz, Theo Holt-Bailey, Preece Killick, Rosie Nicholls, Lee McGovern**

PRODUCTION TEAM

Production Manager	**Simon Sturgess**
Stage Manager	**Sarah Buik**
Deputy Stage Manager	**Natasha Gooden**
Assistant Stage Manager	**Cleo Maynard**

Production photography by **Robert Day** and **Jane Hobson**
Online video footage shot and edited by **Edmund Swabey**
Cover design and concept: **N9 Design**

THANKS TO
Booker Wholesale, Tottenham
Cathall Leisure Centre, Leytonstone
Contacto Limited
Electronic Cigarettes donated by www.ECigaretteDirect.co.uk, the Smoker's Angels
Industrial Plastic Supplies Ltd
Phones 4U
Sheila's Florist, Leytonstone Road, www.sheilasflorist.com

CAST

Ashley Campbell
Frankie/Moses

Ashley Campbell trained at the Sylvia Young Theatre School and Arts Educational
Theatre credits include:
Five Guys Named Moe (20th Anniversary Production), *High Heel Parrotfish* (**Theatre Royal Stratford East**), *Street Scene* (**Théâtre du Châtelet**, Paris, **Gran Teatre del Liceu**, Barcelona), *The Colored Museum* (**The Victoria and Albert Museum**), *Tick Tick Boom* (**The Union**), *Six Degrees of Separation* (**The Old Vic**), *Little Fish* (**Finborough Theatre**), *Jack and The Beanstalk* (**Barbican**), *The Rat Pack* (UK, European and USA tour), *Bomb-Bitty of Errors* (**West End**), *The Ruffian on the Stair* (**Barons Court**), *Fame* (UK tour, West End), *Carousel* (**National Theatre**), *Carmen Jones* (**Old Vic**).
Film credits include: JAM
Television credits include:
Stories from the Heart, Hollyoaks Later, Hollyoaks, Holby City, Ultimate force, William and Mary, The Mysti Show, Bard 2 Verse, Let's Write a Story.
Radio credits include:
Mogadishu.
Later this year Ashley will join the company of the original London cast of *The Color Purple* at **The Menier Chocolate factory**.

Jennifer Daley
Lucy Lockwood

Jennifer trained at the Webber Douglas Academy of Dramatic Art and Middlesex University
Theatre credits include:
Bashment (**Theatre Royal Stratford East**), *Cymbeline, Kiss Me Like You Mean It, Love You Too* (**Soho Theatre**), *Taken In* (**Drill Hall**), *The South London Passion Plays* (**Tristan Bates**).
Film credits include: *Fit, Fifteen Stories, Swim* and the film adaptation of *Bashment*, for which she won the **Best Supporting Actress Award** at the **British Independent Film Festival**
Television credits include:
EastEnders, Casualty, Doctors, Dalziel and Pascoe, Hidden Lives
Jennifer plays the role of Amy Franks in the popular long-running soap *The Archers* on **BBC Radio 4**.

James Farrar
Matthew Prospect

James trained at the Royal Central School of Speech and Drama

Theatre credits include: *Othello's Revenge* (**Gasteig**, Munich), *Bin Men* (**Hen & Chickens**), *The Investigation* (**Arcola**)

Film credits include: *Donkey*, *Dominic*

Television credits include: *Hollyoaks*

James plays the lead role of David in the short film *Donkey* which won the **2012 Critics Choice Award** at **Tribeca Film Festival**.

Frankie Fitzgerald
Mark Prospect

Frankie trained at the Webber Douglas Academy of Dramatic Art

Theatre credits include: *Slap* (**Theatre Royal Stratford East**), *Pools Paradise* (UK tour), *A Midsummer Night's Dream* (**Millpond Media**), *Scripted Away* (**Warehouse Theatre**).

Film Credits Include: *Krish and Lee* (Jaffa Films), *Stormhouse* (Scanner Rhodes), *Troy* (Warner Brothers), *Banana Chocolate* (Short), *London Love Story* (Short)

Television credits include: *Holby City, The Impression Show, He Kills Coppers, Hotel Babylon, Dream Team, The Stepfather, Casualty, EastEnders.*
www.frankiefitzgerald.co.uk

Sasha Frost
Janine Lockwood-Prospect

Sasha trained at The Liverpool
Institute for Performing Art
(LIPA)
Theatre credits include:
Suspension (**Bristol Old
Vic**), *The Canterville Ghost*
(**Southwark Playhouse**), *Home*
(**Tristan Bates Theatre**),
Brezhnev's Children (**BAC**).
Film credits include: *FIT*, *Kick-
Off*.
Television credits include:
*Frankie, Doctors, Privates,
Garrow's Law, Holby City,
Hollyoaks*.

Louise Jameson
Bridie Prospect

Louise trained at RADA and soon
after joined the Royal Shakespeare
Company for two years
Television series credits include:
*Dr Who, Emmerdale, Omega
Factor, Rides, The Secret Diary
of Adrian Mole, Bergerac, River
City, EastEnders*, her personal
favourite *Tenko*, and most recently
Doc Martin.
Film credits include: *My Friend
Walter, Stick With Me Kid, Run For
Your Wife*, award winning *Cleaning
Up* and a short to be released this
year, *Charity*.
In the last twelve months Louise
has played Jocasta in *Oedipus*
with Steven Berkoff's company,
and appeared in *Doctors, Holby
City* and *The Dumping Ground*.
She and her writing partner, Nigel
Fairs, have just completed a tour
of their play *My Gay Best Friend*
which won the People's Choice
award at the Brighton Festival, and
her one-woman show *Pulling Faces*
(a comedy about the dilemma of
whether to go under the knife)
written by Helen Goldwyn. Louise
writes, directs and performs for
audio company Big Finish. Her
first children's book, *Beware the
Goblin Men*, is being published
in November by Upstage and her
next job is filming another short,
The Masnavi Algorithm. She lives
in the heart of Kent, runs her own
company (tlc productions) and a
fringe venue (at The Beacon) but
considers her two sons to be her
best productions to date.
www.louisejameson.com

Gavin McCluskey
John Prospect

Gavin trained at CPA Studios
Theatre credits include: *She Loves Me* for Stephen Mear (**Minerva Theatre, Chichester Festival Theatres**), *The Silver Sword* (Rehearsed reading, **Hackney Empire**), *Chitty Chitty Bang Bang* (**London Palladium**).
Film credits include: Lucas in *Ceop – First to a Million*.
Singer/songwriter credits include: *Roads* for *Deaf Men Dancing* performed at the Sense of Freedom Festival (**The Place Theatre**, London). Gavin is currently in the process of recording his new EP.
Commerical credits include: Childline/NSPCC and Northern Bank.

Dominique Moore
Sunai Suleyman

Dominique trained at Sylvia Young Theatre School
Theatre credits include: *Bedwas Boy/Mandela* (**Chapter Arts Centre**, Cardiff), *Blaggers* (**Catford Theatre**), *Aladdin* (**Lyric Hammersmith**), *Rough Cuts* (**The Arts Theatre**), *Megamix* (**The Royal Albert Hall**), *The Lion King* (original London cast), *Hey Mr Producer* (**Lyceum Theatre**, West End), *Whistle Down The Wind* (**Aldwych Theatre,** West End), *Annie* (**Victoria Palace**, West End), *Oliver!* (**London Palladium,** West End).
Film credits include: *The Physician.*
Television credits include: *Quick Cuts, Horrible Histories, Watson & Oliver, Phoneshop, Gagstars, Hotel Trubble, The Outsiders, Hounded, My Almost Famous Family, Movie Surfers, Life Bites, Kings Of London, Empty, Barely Legal, Dis/ Connected, Little Miss Jocelyn, Lil Sisters, Footballers Wives Extra Time, Stupid, Casualty, The Crust, U Get Me, Fur TV, The Queens Nose, The Bill, Paddington Green, Get Up Stand Up.*
Online credits include: Donna Rush, Keep Quiet and Nothing Changes, The Fleet, My Almost Famous Family Interactive.

Jamie Nichols
Luke Prospect

Jamie trained at Boden Studios, London

Theatre credits include: *The Wedding Singer – The Musical* (**Millfield Theatre**), *Eurobeat – Almost Eurovision* (**Millfield Theatre**) *Jesus Christ Superstar* (**Wyllyotts Theatre**).

Television credits include: *Life Begins, The Bill, EastEnders, The Last Detective, Britain's Secret Shame.*

Film credits include: *Peekabo* (**Urban Myth Productions**), *Wickham Road* (**Northiam Films**).

In addition to working as an actor, Jamie is also an Agent in the industry. He sends special thanks to Joanne McLintock and obviously his Mum!

CREATIVE TEAM

Rikki Beadle-Blair
Writer & Director

Like the characters in *Gutted*, Rikki Beadle-Blair is a South East Londoner. He is also a writer, director, composer, choreographer, designer, producer and performer. He has won several awards including the **Sony Award**, the **Los Angeles Outfest Screenwriting** and **Outstanding Achievement Awards**. His projects include several feature films and TV series, including *Stonewall* for the BBC, *Metrosexuality* for Channel 4, *Noah's Arc* for MTV LOGO in the USA as well as *FIT, KickOff* and *Bashment* for his own company Team Angelica. Currently shooting in the US is his latest screenplay *Blackbird*, directed by award-winning independent filmmaker Patrik Ian Polk. Rikki also works extensively in theatre and has written 28 plays in the last decade including four for **Theatre Royal Stratord East**: *Bashment, Familyman, Shalom Baby* and *Gutted*. He founded Team Angelica in order to create opportunities for actors and creatives in all entertainment fields and is a committed and passionate mentor to artists across the UK, in the US and South Africa.

If you want to work with Rikki, contact rikki@teamangelica.com

Michael Nabarro
Lighting Designer

Michael's recent lighting designs include *Shalom Baby* (**Theatre Royal Stratford East**), *The 14th Tale*, *Black T-Shirt Collection* (**National Theatre** and touring), *Boys* (Headlong, HighTide and **Nuffield**, Southampton), *Untitled* (**Bristol Old Vic**, **Soho Theatre** and touring), *The World's Wife* (**Trafalgar Studios** and touring), *Ghosts in the Gallery* (**Polka Theatre**), *Coming Home*, *The Ballad of Crazy Paola*, *The Lady from the Sea*, *An Enemy of the People* and *The Blind* (**Arcola Theatre**), *Our Share of Tomorrow*, *Lough/Rain*, *Limbo* and *1984* (**York Theatre Royal**), *Slaves*, *Beasts* and *Cocoa* (**Theatre503**).

Michael is a graduate of the RADA Lighting Design course. He previously graduated from Cambridge University and spent three years managing the **ADC Theatre** in Cambridge. Michael is also the Managing Director of Spektrix, a provider of cloud-based ticketing systems to around 120 UK arts organisations.

Theo Holloway
Sound Designer

Theo's recent work as a sound designer includes: *Jack & the Beanstalk*, *Shalom Baby*, *Two Women*, *The Great Extension* and *The Graft* (**Theatre Royal Stratford East**), *Spring Awakening* (UK Tour), *Little Charley Bear and his Christmas Adventure* (**Ambassador's Theatre**), *Whisper Me Happy Ever After* (UK Schools Tour), *The Woman in Black* (UK Tour – Associate Sound Designer), *Macbeth* (UK Tour), *The Trojan War & Peace* Season, *The Dangerous Journeys* Season, *The Bad Boys* Season (**The Scoop**, London), *The Producers* (**Yvonne Arnaud Theatre**), *Men are from Mars, Women are from Venus* (UK Tour), *Third Floor* (**Trafalgar Studios 2**), *The Moon is Halfway to Heaven* (**Jermyn Street Theatre**), *Parade* (**Southwark Playhouse**), *Macbeth* (UK Tour), *Sign of the Times* (**Duchess Theatre** – Musical Arrangements), *The Knitting Circle* (**Soho Theatre**), *The Invisible Man* (**Menier Chocolate Factory** – Associate Sound Designer), *Hamlet* (UK Tour), *Pam Ann – Flying High* (**Vaudeville Theatre**), *Spare* (**New Diorama Theatre**), *Corrie!* (**The Lowry**, Salford), *Counted?* (**London County Hall** – Consultant Sound Designer), *Crossings* (**RichMix** and Tour), *Plague Over England* (**Duchess Theatre**).

Theo also works as a technical consultant and software developer for live sound, specialising in radio frequency engineering.

THEATRE ROYAL STRATFORD EAST STAFF

OUR VISION IS UNLIMITED
BUT OUR FUNDING IS NOT...

Theatre Royal Stratford East believes in the ability of theatre to achieve radical change. We are proud of our capacity to draw such a diverse audience to this much loved venue. We couldn't do it without the generous support of our funders as all charitable organisations are feeling the pinch at present, and here at **Theatre Royal Stratford East** it's no different.

We are increasingly reliant upon sponsorship, memberships, donations and legacies to sustain the world-class work of this unique local theatre. So we would urge you, if you like what you see, to get in touch with us to explore the many ways you can support our on stage work or our inspirational programme for young people and the community.

Supporting our vital work starts from £250 and in return you will receive a partnership that will work for you at every stage, including access to great behind-the-scenes moments and the opportunity to involve any community partners you may have.

We invite you to help us safeguard the future of this inspirational and iconic theatre. For more information on all sponsorships, donations, memberships and legacy, please contact Sarah Sawkins, Head of Development on 020 8279 1137 or email ssawkins@stratfordeast.com

WE WOULD LIKE TO THANK THE
FOLLOWING FOR THEIR SUPPORT

TRUSTS AND FOUNDATIONS
The ACT Foundation, Community Development Foundation, Jack Petchey Foundation, Swan Foundation and The Garrick Club Causes Dear Committee.

MAJOR DONORS
Martina Cole, Elizabeth and Derek Joseph, Lord Tony Hall CBE, Carol Lake, Andrew Cowan, Terry Brown and all those who wish to remain anonymous.

THE VISION COLLECTIVE
Michael and Dianne Bienes, Derek Brown, Barbara Ferris, Nick & Wendy Jakob, Angela & Stephen Jordan, Elizabeth and Derek Joseph, Mansell Bouquet Ltd, Murray Melvin, Carol Murphy, Nick and Wendy Jakob, Stefano Nappo, Sofie Mason, Derek Paget, Toni Palmer, Scrutton Estates Ltd, Gordon Sheret, Jan & Bill Smith, Jane Storie, Lady Stratford, Sabine Vinck, Hedley G Wright and all those who wish to remain anonymous.

BUSINESS SUPPORTERS
The Adam Street Private Members Club, Devonshires Solicitors

We would also like to express our thanks to the Avis Bunnage Estate.

Theatre Royal Stratford East
A People's Theatre

Theatre Royal Stratford East is a prolific developer of new work, attracting artists and audiences often not represented in many other venues. This award-wining theatre, located in the heart of London's East End on the edge of the new Queen Elizabeth Olympic Park, it prides itself on creating world class work that reflects the concerns, hopes and dreams of its community. Through a continuous loop it inspires and is inspired by its vibrant, young and diverse audience.

Contacting Theatre Royal Stratford East
Theatre Royal Stratford East
Gerry Raffles Square
Stratford
London
E15 1BN
www.stratfordeast.com
theatreroyal@stratfordeast.com
Twitter @stratfordeast
Facebook /theatreroyalstratfordeast

Box Office & Information
020 8534 0310 Mon – Sat, 10am – 6pm

Typetalk
07972 918 050

Fax
020 8534 8381

Administration Line
020 8534 7374

Foreword

People say 'Write what you know.' Wise advice, for sure. I believe in writing what you want to know. What inspires me to write a new project are the events, things and people that I initially believe that I don't understand. Then I set off on a journey of self-discovery – searching for my reflection in the faces of people that do and say the things that I believe I would never say or do, seeking my connection. In them I excavate my addictions and my contradictions. Through them I find my connection to every livinddg soul and find the courage to confront my complex humanity.

GUTTED is a play I have waited my life to write. Or rather to write itself. My first plays, written at the age of seven, scribbled on paper scrounged from the paper factory on Bermondsey Street were made up for my friends to perform at the bottom of the stairs of our council block on White's Grounds Estate. Then, as now, I cast first and then wrote with the voices of my actors in mind, finding ways to represent them, whilst pushing and stretching them into characters – all the while pushing, stretching and representing myself. It was there I learned to tell people stories without judgement, it was then I discovered the thrill of getting out of my own way and allowing their rhythms, their poetry and passions to possess my pen. That was how I got hooked on the rush of connection – with characters, with performers, with audience.

And this is what has led me here – almost half a decade later – to you, with this offer. To take my outstretched hand and come witness these events, to spend time together with these simple complicated people, share their epic untidy everyday emotions, experience their ugly, lovely mistakes and perhaps see and hear glimpses of our own faces and voices. To find family we never knew we had. To connect.

Rikki Beadle-Blair, April 2013

If you want to work with Rikki, please email rikki@teamangelica.com

Rikki Beadle-Blair

GUTTED

OBERON BOOKS
LONDON

WWW.OBERONBOOKS.COM

First published in 2013 by Oberon Books Ltd
521 Caledonian Road, London N7 9RH
Tel: +44 (0) 20 7607 3637 / Fax: +44 (0) 20 7607 3629
e-mail: info@oberonbooks.com
www.oberonbooks.com

A catalogue record for this book is available from the British Library.

PB ISBN: 978-1-78319-016-4
E ISBN: 978-1-78319-515-2

Cover design by N9 Design
Production photography by Robert Day

Author photograph by Gary Beadle

Printed, bound and converted
by CPI Group (UK) Ltd, Croydon, CR0 4YY.

Visit www.oberonbooks.com to read more about all our books and to buy them. You will also find features, author interviews and news of any author events, and you can sign up for e-newsletters so that you're always first to hear about our new releases.

For Robert Chevara:
South London Skylark, friend, fellow warrior,
inspiration, brother

Thanks: to the Actor's Centre, the Tristan Bates Theatre, Joni Levinson, Johnny Gordon, Dee-Dee Samuel, Kfir Yefet, Robert Chevara, Pam Callahan, Lois Acton, David Squire and Gil Berry, with extra special thanks to the amazing Marcia Battise, Carleen Beadle, Joel Dommett, Berri George, Ed Swabey, Adam Foster, Ian David Holmes, Marissa Joseph, Helen Sheals, Luke Toulson, Joe Marshall, Jason Maza, Ethoseia Hylton, Toby Wharton, John Samuel Worsey, Helen Worsey, Patrick Molyneux, Richard, Darren & Anthony, the cast of *Sweet* and *Laters* and all of Team Angelica for helping me develop this play.

Characters

BRIDIE PROSPECT
50-something: Irish ancestry, tough, shrewd, old-school
Bermondsey. The Queen of the South-London council estates;
her sons all princes and knights.

MATTHEW PROSPECT
Eldest son. 26. 1st Division footballer, lean,
focused, haunted, damaged.

MARK PROSPECT
Second eldest, 24. Market stall holder. Loud, sociable,
passionately dependable family man. Loyal and lethal as a pit-
bull. Worships his wife and twin five-year-olds.

LUKE PROSPECT
Third eldest. 22. Entrepreneur. Independent. Materialistic.
Ambitious. Aspires to Brad Pitt in *Oceans 11* – defaults to Brad Pitt
in *Fight Club*. Loves trans-ladies.

JOHN PROSPECT
The youngest. 20, Unemployed. Passionate, angry,
aggressive, deeply wounded. Converted to Islam.

LUCY LOCKWOOD
28, Matthew's girlfriend. Black/Mixed-race. Sleek.
High-maintenance. Intense. Beautiful. Broken.

JANINE LOCKWOOD-PROSPECT
29, Mark's wife. Black/mixed-race.
Luscious. Kittenish, loud, volatile.

SUNAI SULEYMAN
20, John's girl. Black African Muslim parentage
and up-bringing. Composed. Smart. Loving. Strong.

FRANKIE
Indeterminate age, Black/Mixed-race, Pre-operative male to
female transsexual. Elegant but down to earth. Wary. Strong.

MOSES
(Can be played by the actor who plays FRANKIE) 16, Black. Sexy.
'Cool.' Swagga. Hypermasculine. Smooth talker.
Young offender. Top dog.

The story is set in Bermondsey. There is some contemporary 'blackney' slang thrown in but (Moses excepted) all the characters speak with broad strong Cockney-influenced 'sarf-east' London accents.

However, I'm happy for the play to be performed with entirely different accents, whether it be Liverpool or Chicago, or Australia or Ireland and the slang to be translated as necessary… But I ask the exploration of working-class language and rhythm be respected.

A seamless flow of scenes whenever possible.

NOW – MATTHEW'S ROOM – REHAB CLINIC

MATTHEW packing his bag – emptying it – repacking it.

MATTHEW's mobile rings.

MATTHEW: Fuck!

> *(Pacing feverishly.)* Fuck fuck fuck fuck fuck fuck fuck fuck fuck fuck fuck…

He empties his bag, hurling each thing away. A shirt. A tracksuit. A copy of Peter Pan, a toothbrush, a razor…

My name is Matthew Patrick Prospect – I'm eleven years old and I have legs.

He pulls out a pair of running shoes – puts them on.

Legs that can speak – legs that fly – I am my legs. They're all that's real about me. They're all anyone can trust.

He starts a training warm-up…

It takes a thousand begs – a thousand notes from school – to get Dad to come down to see the school team – and when he sees me – he almost spills his tin. I know he's watching and I am fucking flying and when I hear him cheering I am in fucking orbit…I'm watching the earth from the air and it is fucking beautiful and I am in wonder – shit, to think I used to live there…before I was a star.

MATTHEW runs.

Thirteen years old. And I am running – round the park doing sprints while Dad spits commands and hatches plans for my future. Fifteen years old – I am running – pounding roads in the early morning winter dark, a place where Dad won't follow me, where I can hear my own plans, where I can't see Dad's life eating him alive. Seventeen years old and I am running all the way into the first division. Running right through to twenty-one and running on the spot by the bench – trying to keep warm in case I get the chance to play. Twenty-two, twenty three – running down the white lines running from the years before – crimes I've committed, damage I've done – all the way to rehab. Twenty-five years – twenty-six – dead on my feet – but legs are all that's left – all that's real. I am my legs. And so. I. Run.

The phone stops. MATTHEW stops.

My name is Matthew Patrick Prospect and I swear to tell the truth, the whole truth and nothing but the truth…so help me…God.

He drops into press-ups…

One! Two! Three! Four! Five!

10 YEARS AGO: FOOTBALL PITCH

MATTHEW is teaching JOHN press-ups.

MATTHEW: *(With ease.)* …fourteen!

JOHN: *(Struggling)* …eight!

MATTHEW: fifteen! Catch up! Sixteen!

JOHN: *(Fading.)* Nine… Ten…

MATTHEW: *(Pumping 'em out.)* One two three four five six seven eight nine ten… you will…

JOHN: *(Collapsing.)* Shit man! How do you do that? I wanna do that, man!

MATTHEW: …twelve, thirteen – When you stop whining and start training – sixteen!

JOHN: Yeah, but when, man?

JOHN: Can't I just close my eyes and wake up as you? How's it feel to be you?

MATTHEW: Dunno – too busy training to think about it.

JOHN: …All the girls wanting to shag you – all the blokes are wanting to fight you – and Millwall waiting to sign you the day you hit sixteen.

MATTHEW: …And all it takes…is training.

JOHN drops into press-up position.

JOHN: One! Two! Three! Four! Five!

NOW – HOSPITAL RECEPTION

MARK on his mobile, LUKE reading, BRIDIE snatching drags on the cigarette she hides under her seat, JOHN doing press-ups.

JOHN: …sixteen! seventeen!

BRIDIE: Fuck's sake, will you knock it on the head?

MARK: S' gone to ansaphone… John, man… Leave it out, yeah?

JOHN: Twenty. Third Set! *(Up and panting.)* …'Time?

> *MARK still on the phone, holds out his watch, JOHN glances at it in passing… After a pause he says…*

Forty seconds! Yes!

MARK: Alright, Boss, it's me. We're down in the reception, yeah, just wondering where the fuck you're at, bruv. Alright, laters, yeah?

BRIDIE: Tell him hospitals give me the bleeding creeps.

> *MARK hangs up.*

BRIDIE: Oh, this is bollocks. We should just go in and get him. He's our'n ain't he? *(Pause.)* I'm gonna get him.

> *She starts off.*

MARK/JOHN: I'll go.

> *They overtake her. At that moment MATTHEW enters – he has his bag with him – there is a moment of silence.*

MARK: Alright, boss?

LUKE/JOHN: Alright?

MATTHEW: Alright?

BRIDIE: You'll be alright when I get you home. You kissing or'm I begging?

> *MATTHEW kisses her on the cheek.*

MARK: Right! Motor's outside!

MATTHEW: I'm gonna run.

BRIDIE: Do what?

MATTHEW: I'm gonna run. You go in the car, I'll meet you.

BRIDIE: It's five fucking mile! You know everyone's waiting for you?

MATTHEW: I'll be there. I just need to run.

JOHN: We'll run with you, Bruv, yeah?

MARK: Like back in the day, yeah?

BRIDIE: Don't know what day you're talking about but I'm buggered if I'm doing any running.

LUKE: Right. I'll drive Mum.

He steps forward to take MATTHEW's bag. MATTHEW won't let go.

Bruv?

MATTHEW lets go of the bag.

It's safe, bruv. We going?

MARK: *(Throwing him the keys.)* Marksgetsetgo!

NINE YEARS AGO – BEDROOM

MATTHEW, MARK, LUKE and JOHN stand together, hands held aloft.

MARK: Marksgetsetgo!

They start furiously race-wanking – faces contorting.

JOHN: Shit!

MARK: Already, y' bastard?

JOHN: Shit!

MATTHEW, MARK & LUKE: Bastard!

They wank faster.

JOHN: Skin's still too fucking tight, man!

MATTHEW: I told you peel it back in the bath.

JOHN: I done that!

MATTHEW: You gotta get the foreskin warm, yeah?

JOHN: I done that!

MATTHEW: …then you stretch it, yeah – like this, yeah?

JOHN: I fucking done all that and it's still too fucking tight!

LUKE: Aaaaahhhhh!

MATTHEW, MARK and JOHN dodge LUKE's come.

MATTHEW, MARK & JOHN: Shit!

LUKE: Reach, man, reach!

MATTHEW: Call that reach?

MARK: Watch your fucking eye before I blind ya!

>*MATTHEW and MARK come.*

MATTHEW: Yesss! Yesssss, man!

MARK: Cheating bastard, you flicked it!

MATTHEW: 'kin turbo powerrrrr!

>*JOHN is angrily shoving his dick away.*

MARK: You alright there John, mate? Want me to finish you off, man?

JOHN: Fuck off, will ya? It's alright for you, your dick ain't strangling itself.

MARK: Mine's just weighing me down, mate.

JOHN: Alright, you really need to fuck off…

MARK: Alright, Bruv, keep your toys in your pram!

>*JOHN stomps off…*

LUKE: It's only a wank, bruv!

MATTHEW: Leave him.

LUKE: AAAAAAAAHHHHH!

>*LUKE comes again. MARK and MATT stare at him.*

NOW – STREET

MATTHEW, MARK and JOHN run – MARK struggles to breathe…

JOHN: 'Zat your breathing, bruv?

>You sound like a fucking Hoover!

MARK: Fuck off you little cunt. I'm just getting in the zone.

JOHN: Yeah – fucking heart-failure zone.

MARK: It's Her Indoors, man, I swear. *(Patois.)* Treat me belly too nice, innit?

JOHN: Soul food overload, man?

MARK: That shit's *evil*, man! Fried chicken, fried pigfoot, fried saltfish, fried dumpling… No wonder Jamaica's so chilled out – they can't fucking move! You should see what she's got sorted for you – She's been cooking for a week – S'like fucking carnival back there, man. I told her you'd be going straight back into training, Mattman – she's just kissed her teeth at me.

(Looking at MATTHEW.) How's it feel to be heading for an hero's welcome?

JOHN: Got the whole estate waiting for you, mate. Banner and everything.

MARK: You're the scam-master, mate. Soccer's new wild man – Beat the system, shafted the FA – Nine months paid holiday, y'cunt!

JOHN: Faked a mental breakdown to hide his nasty little coke habit, y'cunt!

MARK: Oy! I thought your people didn't swear, y'cunt? Or ain't we on the Islam this week? I tell you Matt, mate, it's been off the fuckin' hook since you've been gone, man – I can't get this one to eat or drink or have a laugh.

JOHN: Eat pig or drink booze or sniff coke or shag slags.

MARK: Where's your fucking plot, bruv? You're John Prospect, one of the Prospect Boys and you don't drink, don't smoke and you don't have sex – what the fuck else is there?

JOHN: The path of the righteous, brother.

MARK: See what I'm dealing with? Matthew man, I am so fucking glad you are back to kick this boy's arse.

MATTHEW does not answer. MARK and JOHN share a look.

JOHN: Mum reckons your scam's backfired. Reckons you went in the loony-bin normal and come out mental.

MATTHEW: Well, can't disappoint your mum, eh? That's practically the law.

JOHN: …Jimmy Break!

He unzips…

Gotta siphon the python…

MARK: Side of the road man? Ain't that in the Koran – thou shalt not expose thy cock in public?

MARK and MATTHEW join him. JOHN ostentatiously shaking his dick…

What the fuck is that, Geeze? You had an accident?

JOHN: Wassamatter, lads? Ain't you seen a work of art before?

MARK: Your cock's done a Kojak!

JOHN: Captain Picard to you, mate.

MARK: Ain't the poor little sod cold without his coat?

JOHN: 'Oy! Less of the little!

MARK: Did it hurt any, bruv?

JOHN: *(Shrug.)* Piece o' piss. Handsome though, ain't he?

MARK: For a little Jewish bloke.

JOHN gives MARK the filthiest look – zips up and walks away. MARK turns with a rueful smile to MATTHEW.

Johnboy! You fucking drama queen!

(Putting his dick away.) Don't act the cunt y' cunt! We gotta arrive together, man – The Prospect Boys, yeah? Together cross the finish line, raised hands! Yeah!

(To the tune of 'you are my sunshine'.)

We are the Prospects –
Beautiful Prospects –
Everyone hates us –
And we don't care!

(Wheezing.) Johnboy! Slow down, y'cunt!

JOHN: Speed up y'cunts!

NOW – CAR

LUKE drives – BRIDIE gazes out of the window.

BRIDIE: Your brother's changed.

LUKE: Everyone's changing, Mum. Cells are perpetually renewed.

BRIDIE: I'm the one you can't be clever with – so don't waste time trying. He's changed. Kids. You're killers. Why didn't you wanna run with your brothers?

LUKE: I ain't a runner, Mum.

BRIDIE: Bollocks.

LUKE: Someone had to drive you.

BRIDIE: Bollocks.

LUKE: Don't try and fathom me out Mum.

BRIDIE: I've stopped that years gone. I just worry now, it's quicker.

What a litter. One son puts hisself in the loony bin on a blag and comes out genuinely mental – another one thinks he's the bloody Ayatollah and this one lives in the fucking twilight zone… *(She knows he's smiling.)* …glad you can laugh about it.

LUKE: I'm happy in the twilight zone – worrying not required.

BRIDIE: …Bollocks.

EIGHT YEARS AGO – CAR PARK

MATTHEW, MARK, LUKE and JOHN survey a row of cars.

MATTHEW: Picked one?

LUKE looks at JOHN.

LUKE: Bruv?

JOHN: The silver one…

MATTHEW: Make your move.

LUKE produces a wrench – and swings it – to be stopped by:

MARK: But!

LUKE & JOHN: What?

MATTHEW: …If you were gonna do a window – you'd do a rear window – so you don't have to sit on the glass…

MARK: …only you're not gonna do a window because this is a TDA and we don't wanna drive around with a draft, so…?

LUKE: So, we're gonna force the door?

MARK produces a screwdriver.

MATTHEW: We're gonna coax the lock…

JOHN takes it, turns to the car…

MARK: But..!

LUKE/JOHN: What?

MATTHEW: Not this lock…why?

JOHN: Er –

MATTHEW: – Think –

JOHN: – Shit car?

LUKE: Too obvious?

MATTHEW: – Look closer –

MARK: Think faster…

MATTHEW: …'should have hit this and run by now…

LUKE: …Low fuel?

JOHN: …Vinyl seats?

MATTHEW: *(Leaning in to point…)* Immobiliser.

    LUKE and JOHN lean in to look…

LUKE & JOHN: Shit.

MATTHEW: …Next.

EIGHT YEARS AGO – BACKSTREET

Police siren.

MATTHEW, MARK and JOHN hurtle in and try to hide.

MATTHEW: Shit!

MARK: Shit shit shit shit shit   JOHN: Oh shit… Oh shit…
shit shit shit shit…   Oh shit…

MATTHEW: Okay – now, this is what we gotta do, yeah? Send Johnboy out there.

JOHN: Out there? You're having a fucking giraffe, intcha?

MATTHEW: You go out there – say you were alone – We get home, get the call – come down the station and get you out bish bosh – sorted. You're under seventeen, bruv – you're a minor! First offence! Crime don't mean time when it's a first offence.

MARK: Matt's just about to turn pro, little man – he'd be fucked.

MATTHEW: Trust me bruv, you can't do time for B&E on a poxy Ford Capri!

    The siren comes closer.

JOHN: If I do it, no more baby bruv, yeah? No more little man shit.

MARK: Whatever you say, little man.

JOHN: Matt! Tell him!

MATTHEW: Blank him, bruv – after this you're for fucking sure a geezer.

JOHN: A geezer?

MATTHEW: *The* geezer!

MATTHEW gives MARK a look.

MARK: …the geezer.

JOHN: Laters, losers!

He heads toward the flashing light with hands up…

The Geezer!

He's gone.

MATTHEW: Laters, little man…

EIGHT YEARS AGO – DETENTION CENTRE VISITING ROOM

JOHN sits one side of the table – BRIDIE on the other.

BRIDIE: What the fuck am I supposed to say? What the fuck am I supposed to say? No son of mine – no one in my family – never before in my life.

JOHN: Dad was a cat burglar 'til he was 22.

BRIDIE: Yeah, but he never got fucking caught, did he? I don't know what to say so I don't want to say nothing. Alright? Nothing.

Silence.

JOHN: Alright.

Silence.

LATER THAT DAY

MATTHEW, MARK and LUKE swagger in.

JOHN: Alright, y'cunts?

MATTHEW/LUKE: Alright Geeze?

MARK: Alright, little man?

JOHN: 'scuse me? *(Hand to ear, indicating the surroundings.)* Ex-fucking-scuse me?

They fall into silence.

MATTHEW: Anyone giving you any shit, let us fucking know, we'll break in here and sort 'em out, alright?

JOHN: They fucking tread light round me mate – They know I'm a Prospect, you know what I'm saying?

MATTHEW, MARK & LUKE: Yeaaahhhhhh!

MATTHEW: Our reputation reach, ain't it?

JOHN: From time! Everybody knows the Prospect Boyz!

MATTHEW: Safe.

LUKE: How was Mum?

JOHN: You know I can handle Mum.

MATTHEW, MARK & LUKE: Yeaaaahhhhhhhh!

MATTHEW: Favourite son!

MARK: Baby of the family…baby geezer.

JOHN: I never told her you sent me out there, you know that, yeah?

MATTHEW: Why didn't you tell us you'd been nicked before, man? We wouldn't have sacrificed you if we'd known you'd end up doing time.

JOHN: Dunno. Just a natural hero. Ain't no thing.

MARK: Ain't like it's a real fucking prison anyway.

JOHN: Piece of piss. 'shit I'm learning, I'll soon be schooling you.

EIGHT YEARS AGO – DETENTION CENTRE DORM AFTER LIGHTS OUT

Boys bed down in a row. Two beds away we can hear one BOY fucking another. JOHN is crying…

JOHN: Hail Mary, full of grace…

BOY GETTING FUCKED: Arrrgghh!

BOY FUCKING: Shut it!

JOHN: Blessed is the fruit of thy womb…

MOSES: Oy! White boy!

JOHN falls silent.

You praying or crying?

JOHN: Who you calling white boy?

MOSES: Looks like white skin catching the light to me over there, man.

JOHN: Nah, man, I'm Irish.

MOSES: Oh yeah?

JOHN: Yeah, bwoy – Black Irish, innit?

MOSES: *(Chuckles.)* Well, you can chat. F' true… How old're you, Irish?

JOHN: Nearly thirteen, innit? How old're are you?

MOSES: Nearly seventeen. I'm telling you, Irish, you better forget about your pretty white virgins, you get me? 'Cause, round here, God's a black man. Ever heard of Allah, Paddy?

JOHN: He's the Paki God, ain't he?

MOSES: He's everyone's God, you know what I'm saying? Black God from the dark continent – made the first man in his image, f'true. Black and beautiful. Like me.

JOHN: *(Laughing uncertainly.)* Like you?

MOSES: *(Standing.)* Well check it, man – ain't I black?

JOHN: Yeah…

MOSES: And ain't I beautiful?

JOHN: Well…

MOSES: It's dark in here… Bro…come closer, yeah, and you'll see…

JOHN doesn't move.

You don't trust me, man? Ain't I trusting you though? Ain't I talking to you like a friend? Ain't I?

JOHN: Yeah.

MOSES: Yeah, I ain't perfect, man, I sin. I know that. But I'm striving, ain't I?

JOHN: I s'pose…

MOSES: What's your name, Black Irish?

JOHN: John.

MOSES: Ah. John the youngest. The one Jesus loved, yeah?
See, I remember my Bible, black Irish – I used to pray to
a blond Jesus myself – And check the hell it brung me to.
You ever felt alone, blood? Miles from your mother, being
held down by strangers and rode like an animal? I have.
I've been taken. I've been used. I had to grow up before
my time. I was lucky though – You have to have a brother
to protect you inna this here Babylon. Mine found me
the first day I come here – my brother picked me up – he
saved me – taught me 'bout Allah yeah, made me a man –
and set me free.

JOHN: I already got a brother. I got three. One's eighteen.

MOSES: And where are they now? I'm here, blood. Right here.
And I won't let no strangers invade you. How 'bout you
come lie with me, tonight? And we can make plans, ain't
it? Plan to study the Koran and learn 'bout the all-powerful
all-merciful beautiful black God, yeah? Together, yeah?
And we'll make you a man. Wha' y'say, blood?

JOHN starts to get up.

JOHN: Yeah, man… Seen… What's your name, bro?

MOSES: Moses…

NINE YEARS AGO: BEDROOM

MATTHEW and JOHN wanking…

JOHN: *(Struggling with the foreskin trouble.)* Shit! Fuck it!

MATTHEW: Use more oil on it, yeah?

JOHN: I am!

MATTHEW: Well use more!

JOHN: I fucking am! I can hardly hold the greasy fucker
already! It's like a fucking mackerel!

MATTHEW: Okay, stop moving your hand, yeah? Just hold it.

JOHN does so.

Now grip it gently… Move your hand a tiny bit, yeah good, now grip it a bit more so the skin comes back a fraction, now a bit more 'til it hurts, yeah…yeah?

JOHN: *(Sharp intake of breath.)* Shit! Yeah…

MATTHEW: Easy, yeah? Just there yeah – where you can feel it but you can bear it, yeah? Get used to it – relax into the pain, yeah? Yeah?

JOHN: Fuck man, it stings…

MATTHEW: Then ease off a bit then build up again, yeah?

JOHN: Yeah… Fuck! I'm losing it! Shit!

MATTHEW: Losing what? You gonna come?

JOHN: No! My fucking horn! I'm losing my fucking… Shit! This is fuckeries! What's the point in having a cock if it don't fucking work? Even girls can piss without one!

MATTHEW: It works, mate, believe! Mine was like yours – I just had to work at it, that's all. Look…

(Demonstrates on himself.) Grip it just enough, then move your hand just enough so that you feel something… Yeah? Go on, hold mine, man…

JOHN looks at him.

JOHN: Yours, man?

MATTHEW: Yeah, mine, man, don't worry won't bite…

As JOHN reaches out…

…might spit – won't bite…

JOHN pulls his hand back, MATTHEW laughs…

…go on, son…there you go…

JOHN reaches out and holds his brother's dick.

…gently, yeah – now move it yeah – just a fraction, yeah, just a fraction, yeah, 'til the foreskin gets looser, yeah, more, yeah, more yeah… More yeah – that's it, yeah… Yeah, yeah, yeah…

(Comes.) Yeeeeeaahhhhhhhhh…!

(Pause. Then smiles.) See, you're a natural wanker.

He winks.

EIGHT YEARS AGO – DETENTION CENTRE VISITING ROOM

BRIDIE and JOHN sit in silence as before. She gets to her feet.

BRIDIE: See you next week, son.

> *She leaves. JOHN sits alone…*

EIGHT YEARS AGO – DETENTION CENTRE EXERCISE YARD

MOSES and JOHN lifting weights.

MOSES: You want me to speak to her, bro?

JOHN: You don't know my old girl – you can't just talk to her.

MOSES: She's like you then, yeah?

JOHN: Wha' you sayin'? You know you can talk to me.

> *MOSES' face says everything.*

> Look, I just don't listen to people who don't know how to talk. You know how to talk, innit?

MOSES: *(Nodding.)* F'true…

JOHN: F'true! I swear, boy, you can *preach*. And listen. She don't listen. Conversation with her's a one-way street. We're all just road-kill. She mows me down. And the silence is worse. Mum's silence. S'fucking crippling. Like napalm, man – strafes and burns.

MOSES: 'Strafes?' 'nother new word?

JOHN: You know…

> *(Makes the sound of machine gunfire.)* Strafes. My brother Luke always says, 'Assimilate a new word every week and casually work it into conversation wherever possible…' I never listened to him before. I never went in the library before I come in here. I never wanted to participate in a conversation before.

> *MOSES drapes an arm over JOHN's shoulders reassuringly.*

MOSES: You got a smart brother. You're lucky.

> *(As he takes his arm away he pats JOHN's bum.)* And so's he…

JOHN: Thanks for saving me, bro – you know what…?

MOSES: Don't say it.

JOHN: Say what?

(Reddening.) Why not?

MOSES: Only batty boys say it out loud.

JOHN: Batty boys?

MOSES: Benders. Queerboys.

JOHN: My brothers say I love you all the time.

MOSES: *(Smiles.)* I ain't that kind of brother.

JOHN: I dunno – You're closer than you think, I reckon. So when we gonna start studying the Koran, brother?

MOSES: Soon as we learn Arabic, brother.

JOHN: So let's learn Arabic, brother.

JOHN's eye catches someone staring.

Who the fuck you looking at?

(Stepping up and fronting.) Yeah, wha? What? Wha' y' saying? Bring it on!

MOSES comes up to stand behind JOHN.

MOSES: Problem?

The starer moves on past, JOHN and MOSES eyes following…

JOHN: That's it yeah, keep it moving…

(Kisses his teeth.) Pussy-raas, batty boy, queer…

NOW – OUTSIDE THE ESTATE

LUKE is waiting on the corner – talking on his phone.

LUKE: Alright? I'm Bermondsey Lenny. White-face, black pace…bit of Geezer and a total gentlemen – and hotter than a pistol thanks to you. I ain't Brad Pitt – I'm fitter… I ain't Tom Cruise – I'm taller… And I ain't Paul Newman – I'm younger. I'm seeking for a lady with a past, a present and a future and a 38-calibre smile. If you're willing to walk the wire with no net – I'm your safest bet. And remember, when you die, it's only what you didn't do you regret!

(Starts to walk…) 07770333500, Call me, yeah…?

Hanging up as MATTHEW, MARK and JOHN run past, LUKE joins them.

What took you, Y'wankers!

MARK & JOHN: Tosserrrrrrr!

MARK: Everybody waiting for us back at the flats, bruv?

LUKE: Whole estate in its entirety, bruv.

MARK: Hero's welcome, Geeze?

LUKE: Hero's welcome, Geeze!

MARK: Hear that Mattman? Hero's welcome. Whole fucking
estate – every cunt what ever knew us, looked at us,
dreamed of fighting or fucking us waiting there with the
South London Press, for the Prospect Boys to reach home…

(Singing…) We are the Prospects –
Beautiful Prospects…

MARK & LUKE: *Everyone hates us*
And we don't care!

MARK, LUKE & JOHN: *No fucker gets us*
They just respect us…

MATTHEW, MARK, LUKE & JOHN: Please don't take our
prospects away!

YEEEEEEEEEAAAAAAAAAAAAAAAAAAAHHH!!!

NOW – ROCKINGHAM ESTATE

Balloons and streamers around a welcome home banner.

*JOHN stands aside and watches as his brothers hug and wrestle happily
with MATTHEW, popping champagne and terrace-chanting.*

BRIDIE: You little toe-rag…! Come here.

She scoops MATTHEW up in her arms and holds him tight –

My first-born…my first-born… Don't care how old you
are, or how big you are – you're never going nowhere
again.

*She reaches out and grips MARK's jacket – she pulls him in…he
joins the embrace…*

Never never never…

LUKE joins the group hug…BRIDIE and JOHN's eyes meet.

EIGHT YEARS AGO – DETENTION CENTRE WAITING ROOM

JOHN and BRIDIE, sitting in silence.

BRIDIE gets up.

BRIDIE: I'll see you next week, son…

JOHN: I come home next week, Mum.

> *She pauses for a minute…*

BRIDIE: I know. I'll see you there.

> *She leaves.*

EIGHT YEARS AGO – DETENTION CENTRE EXERCISE YARD

MOSES and JOHN lifting weights in silence.

JOHN: …and she just says 'I know'. Long mind-fuck silence… and then she goes 'See you at home.'

> *Silence.*

> So we know what that means – that means she ain't coming to pick me up. That means I'm gonna walk into a silent drum…with her sitting there…

> *(Pause)* …silent.

> *(Pause.)* She guts me like a fucking shellfish. Sucks my insides out.

> *He notices MOSES staring off at something.*

> You checking out that new kid?

> *JOHN goes to stand by MOSES, watching with him for a moment.*

> Poor shit-scared little fuck. You want me to talk to him for you? It's cool – I mean, I'm gone next week man, you're gonna need a spar, you think he'd make a good spar?

MOSES: If I wanna talk to him I'll talk to him.

> *(Looking…)* When I'm ready.

JOHN: Yeah, 'cause you can talk, man. And I ain't gone yet. We still got 'nuff conversations in us. Like, for instance you never taught me the Koran like you promised. We never learned Arabic. We should get a book – we should learn Arabic.

MOSES: In a week?

JOHN: 'Nuff things happen in a week. If we learned Arabic – the screws wouldn't know what the fuck we were talking about – it could be our own private language we can talk about the Jihad right in front of the white devil – we can explore the Koran. So if you talked to Mum – for me – what would you say?

MOSES: Fuck's sake, man, will you shut the fuck up? I don't know nothing about no Koran. I just like fucking white boys.

Pause – MOSES moves away calling to the new boy…

Hey! White boy!

JOHN: *(Quiet.)* Who you calling white boy?

EIGHT YEARS AGO – DETENTION CENTRE DORMITORY

JOHN is crying by the light of a torch, as he takes off a sock. He takes a box of nails and empties it into the sock. He twists the top of the sock. He creeps over to where MOSES is sleeping and whispers, still crying…

JOHN: You promised…

With one swing JOHN hits MOSES in the head with the sock. MOSES utters the smallest gasp – he does not move. JOHN is still crying as he empties out the sock – and puts it back on, then whispers…

(Tenderly.) I love you, bro…

And crawls back to bed, still crying…

EIGHT YEARS AGO – DETENTION CENTRE VISITING ROOM

JOHN sits looking at the ground as MATTHEW, MARK and LUKE arrive – the swaggering subdued.

MATTHEW: Bruv…

MARK: Bruv…

LUKE: Bruv…

They sit – silent.

MATTHEW: So, what the fuck, bruv? Don't you ever wanna come home or what?

JOHN shrugs.

MARK: Sounds like you fucked that kid up for real, though.

JOHN: Yeah, man, for real.

MARK: He ain't gonna be messing with no Prospect boy from the fucking hospital, Geeze, know what I mean?

LUKE: What did he try to do to you, Johnboy?

MATTHEW: He try to get queer on you, man?

> *Silence.*

JOHN: You know he'd be lying in the ground next to Dad if he tried that with me, man.

MARK: Well, it was close, bruv. You took that fucker *out!* Still in intensive care, boy!

MATTHEW/MARK/LUKE: Yeeeahhhh, boyyyyyyeeeee!

MATTHEW: So what he fucking do, man?

JOHN: Oh, you know, man – I dunno man – just…talking shit, know what I mean?

MARK: He call you 'Little man?'

JOHN: Called me white boy.

> *MATTHEW, MARK and LUKE react.*

MARK: Now that's fucked up.

LUKE: Didn't you tell him you were Irish?

MATTHEW: Tell him? He *showed* him, right Johnboy?

JOHN: When's Mum coming?

> *MATTHEW, MARK and LUKE say nothing. JOHN looks at BRIDIE.*

NOW – ROCKINGHAM ESTATE

JOHN, eyes locked with BRIDIE, stands aside watching his brothers and mother embrace.

JOHN: Boss.

> *All turn to look at him.*

> Press wants to talk to you. Over there.

MARK: Want me to tell 'em to fuck off, bruv?

BRIDIE: Tell 'em he'll be there after he's finished reuniting with his friends and family.

(To MATTHEW.) Underarms – now.

MATTHEW: Got my bag, Lukey?

LUKE: Over there, Geeze.

MATTHEW approaches a pile of jackets and coats and searches for his bag…

MARK: I'll go in with you, bruv.

BRIDIE: You stop here – if you follow him they'll think he's on suicide watch.

MARK: Alright, you lot! Ladies and gentlemen, ten minutes, yeah? Beers over there!

As MATTHEW goes into the house a phone rings. He delves into a side pocket of his bag, finds it and answers.

MATTHEW: Hello?

LUKE: *(Hurrying over.)* That's mine, bruv!

LIGHTS UP ON FRANKIE'S HOME.

FRANKIE: Is that Bermondsey Lenny?

Pause, MATTHEW looks at LUKE.

MATTHEW: Hold up…

He holds the phone out…

For you, mate.

LUKE takes his phone.

LUKE: Yeah.

FRANKIE: Sorry, Bermondsey Lenny?

LUKE turns away as casually as possible as MATTHEW leaves.

LUKE: Speaking.

FRANKIE: Hello. You left me a voicemail answering my ad?

LUKE: Oh, yeah, cool… How you doing?

FRANKIE: Nervous. Excited.

LUKE: Yeah, cool – tell you what, yeah, how about if I bell you back?

FRANKIE: Oh. Okay.

LUKE: *(Checking the display.)* I'll be able to get you on this number for a while yeah?

FRANKIE says nothing.

(A touch more gently.) Look – It's cool, yeah? I'm gonna call you. …Sweet.

LUKE hangs up. Lights down on FRANKIE.

SEVEN YEARS AGO – ELEPHANT & CASTLE SUPER BOWL

MATTHEW and MARK check out LUCY and JANINE – in the next lane.

MARK: Sweeeet, man…

MATTHEW: Sweeeet. Mine is *tight*, man!

MARK: Mine is well lush. She's fucking tropical. What is it 'bout sistas, bruv?

MATTHEW: It's everything.

ROCKINGHAM ESTATE – NOW

JOHN goes through a whole cigarette really really fast – binge-smoking. He knocks it back with a drink… He starts to choke… Pulling himself together he turns back to join the party…to find himself face to face with SUNAI – a beautiful black girl about his age – 20. She holds a large punch-bowl. They face each other down…

JOHN: What you doing here?

SUNAI: Your mum asked me.

JOHN: Yeah, my mum – not yours, alright?

SUNAI: Johnny…don't.

JOHN: 'she sighed patiently…'

SUNAI: If you want me to go you can just ask me to go.

JOHN: 'she said, acting all wounded to attack.' If you want me to fuck off you can just say fuck off.

BRIDIE: Fuck off.

They turn to find BRIDIE standing there.

Oops-a-daisy, I thought you was talking to me. Am I interrupting summink? Well, Burton and Taylor, it'll have to wait, the sweaty masses are waiting for their punch. See you over there, Sunai, yeah?

SUNAI takes the punch over.

JOHN: Stay out of it, Mum. It's nothing to do with you.

BRIDIE: I know love. That's why I invited her.

BRIDIE turns on her heel and moves on…

TWO YEARS AGO – JOB CENTRE

SUNAI and JOHN face each other over a desk.

SUNAI: *(Laughing.)* What did you say?

JOHN: You heard me…

(Leans in close.) A salaam-alaiku, sister…

He grins at her.

SUNAI: What do you know about 'A salaam-alaiku?'

JOHN: Plenty. Prob'ly could teach you a little sumpin' sumpin'…

SUNAI: You can't even say it.

JOHN: Then maybe you can teach me.

SUNAI: This look like a mosque to you?

JOHN: A mosque is wherever you make it, Sister Suleyman.

Instinctively she covers her name-tag – realises the pointlessness of her action – picks up her pen. He leans back in his seat, chewing…

Sunai Suleyman. Nice Muslim name. Miss?

She looks down… He smiles…

…Miss.

SUNAI: Address?

JOHN: 123 Snowfields Estate.

SUNAI: Postcode SE1…?

JOHN: 1… 4… U.

SUNAI: Sex…

JOHN: …Yes please…

SUNAI: …male.

JOHN: You noticed. Can I expect the personal touch?

SUNAI: Round here the personal touch is a swift slap.

JOHN: Hands-on approach, yeah?

SUNAI: Are you always like this?

JOHN: No. You've changed me.

SUNAI: Mr Prospect, you live on a council estate south of the Elephant and Castle and are far too well-dressed for someone claiming to be long-term unemployed. Why would a nice Muslim girl wanna go out with someone like you?

JOHN: Go out? With someone like me? Now there's an idea… 'cause I'm the one, sister.

A MONTH LATER

JOHN and SUNAI walking and laughing to the corner.

SUNAI: 'Cause I'm the one, sister'!

JOHN: Well, a brother's gotta have a line, innit?

SUNAI: Well, that certainly was a line.

JOHN: Worked, didn't it? Here ain't you? A whole month later. I'm all lines round you, girl. I got chat coming out me arse.

(*Seeing her face.*) Bum. Bottom.

(*Teasing.*) Arse.

SUNAI: Johnny!

JOHN: What are you gonna do when our kids come home effing and blinding?

SUNAI: I'll say, 'I don't know where you got that from.' Certainly not me and your dad.

JOHN: And if that don't   SUNAI: Johnny!
work I'll slap the shit out
of 'em. It's cool, Sister
Suleyman, your kids're
safe with me… The lion
is a lamb in the spell of
your kiss.

SUNAI: I live round the corner, Johnny – what if one of my brother's comes past and sees me kissing…

JOHN: A white boy? …an infidel?

SUNAI: …anyone.

JOHN: I ain't anyone sister, I'm *the* one.

SUNAI kisses him quickly on the cheek…and pulling on her head-scarf, hurries home… JOHN watches her every step.

NOW – ROCKINGHAM ESTATE

JANINE and MARK, nursing plastic champagne glasses. MARK yells at some kids offstage.

MARK: Paris – will you stop creating! Come on, man, she can't hurt you – she's only a girl! Persephone! Leave your brother alone, or no Chupa-Chups on the way home you get me? Persephone! Paris!

JANINE: *(Turning on them.)* You lot!

They stop dead.

Yes. That's what I'm talking about. Keep it down.

(Offering MARK her cheek.) Alright, gangsta?

MARK: Wha'y'sayin', Gangsta bitch?

JANINE: So you lot ran home from Balham?

MARK: What can I say? Y' man *fit!*

JANINE: Well, I hope it made you happy – 'cause you lot are sad.

(Thrusting her empty glass at MARK.) Refill.

MARK moves away to the drinks table.

JOHN watches SUNAI pulling on her coat.

JOHN: It won't work, you know. The stalking policy. Just happening to be there – looking all beautiful… I'm past all that now. I see you like you really are.

SUNAI: And what am I really?

JOHN: A whore. A western concubine…

SUNAI: You never called me that when you spent a year trying to get in my knickers.

JOHN: You never explained to me, though, did you?

SUNAI: About what?

JOHN: About right and wrong?

SUNAI: What did I know about right and wrong?

JOHN: More than me – I just knew about wrong, didn't I? You could have taught me instead of tempting me.

SUNAI: Tempting you? I was a virgin, Johnny! I told you all that.

JOHN: Call that telling, do ya? 'Oh Johnny, I've never – Oh Johnny, I can't – Oh Johnny, I want to…'

SUNAI: 'But I can't…'

JOHN: 'I want to…'

SUNAI: 'BUT I CAN'T!'

JOHN: But you did. You fucking let the Western devil in – uncut, unclean, uneducated, unworthy. You threw away the one gift you had to give.

SUNAI: The one gift? Oh, thank you.

JOHN: You know what I mean, Sunai…

SUNAI: Oh thank you! I gave up my family to be with you – I gave up my life!

JOHN: See, that's what you don't understand, woman. Your life ain't your'n to give. You gave up something worth fifty times your life. You gave up our innocence.

SUNAI: I can't believe I'm stood here listening to you tell me how to be a good Muslim girl.

SUNAI: Reverse time? Go back and seal myself up and fight you off and make you marry me? Stop loving you?	JOHN: It's too late for that.

SUNAI: What do you want me to do, Johnny?
Yes, Johnny – it's too fucking late!

JOHN: It's too late…
It's too late…

It's too late…

It's too late…

SUNAI: It's too late, Johnny. I know that. Let's just stop, yeah? Stop all this fighting with ghosts. I'm gonna go. I love you.

SUNAI leaves.

JOHN: *(Quietly.)* Well, don't.

EIGHT MONTHS AGO – BEDROOM

JOHN and SUNAI on his bed. JOHN, excited, eyes closed.

JOHN: Can I open 'em now?

SUNAI: No.

She produces a book in a small sellotaped paper bag.

JOHN: Now?

SUNAI: *(Ripping the bag away.)* No!

She takes both his hands and places the book in them.

Okay… No!

She grabs the books and quickly picks the price off the back…

Wait, wait…

She once again places the book in his hands…

OK.

JOHN keeps his eyes shut. Pause.

OK… You can open your eyes now.

JOHN: It's a book.

SUNAI: …it's more than a book…

JOHN: I don't like books – I'm allergic.

SUNAI: …It's *the* book.

JOHN: *(Opens his eyes.)* Fucking Hell!

(To Heaven.) Sorry Allah! Blimmin' Heck – It's the blimmin' Koran!

He looks up at her, eyes shining – gives her a big kiss.

SUNAI: I got so sick of you asking me questions about it.

JOHN: Oh, babe! Babe!

(Placing the book aside as he kisses her again with growing ardour.)

How can I thank you?

SUNAI: *(Wriggling as she snatches up the book.)* Now now, brother
– let us not stray from the righteous path…

JOHN: What could I possibly give you in return? Mmm!

SUNAI: *(Reading.) 'Menstruation – it is an indisposition. Keep aloof
from women during their menstrual periods…'*

JOHN: *(Grabbing at the Koran.)* Any Kama Sutra tips in there?

SUNAI: *'…and do not touch them 'til they are clean again.'*

JOHN: *'Women are your fields. Go into your fields…as you please…'*
(Kisses her.) 'Allah knows all and hears all.
(Kiss.) He will not call you to account for that which is…
(Kiss.) …inadvert in your oaths.'

SUNAI: *(Wriggling – but not pushing him away…)* Johnny…
Johnny… I can't…

JOHN: You want to.

SUNAI: …But I can't. I shouldn't even be in this room…not
alone…not with a boy like you…

JOHN: Ain't I been a good boy for you, though? Ain't I been
patient over a year? Practically a saint?

SUNAI: There are no saints in the Koran…

JOHN: Ain't no saints on Earth, neither – Not with you to
tempt us. Men are weak. But Allah understands…

SUNAI: Johnny… I should go…

JOHN: But you can't…
(Kiss.) 'Allah is forgiving and lenient…'
As they lay down…
Allah, will forgive…

NOW – ROCKINGHAM ESTATE

MARK is talking to his (unseen) kids, hands behind his back.

MARK: Paris! Persephone! Check this out what I got for you,
yeah?
He produces a pair of filled champagne glasses.

Babycham! That's for being quiet, yeah? That's for being good kids… Shhh!

As they walk away, he notices something…

Seph, babe, wait, babe…

(Pulling back.) What's that? This. On the back of your neck? It looks burnt. Where's your chain? Paris, did you grab your sister's chain? It's cool, I'm not angry – just – if anything's happening at school, you know you can talk to me, yeah? Daddy's got your back. Now, steer clear of Mum with the booze, yeah? Mum ain't the word.

MATTHEW approaches JANINE.

JANINE: Alright, Prodigal boy?

MATTHEW: Alright, Miss Carriage-a-justice?

How's things?

JANINE: Things are what they are, ain't they? You look good.

MATTHEW: You look better.

JANINE: Nothing's changed, then. You ain't gonna ask about my sister, then?

MATTHEW: Why, are you your sister's keeper?

MARK returns with drinks…

MARK: Flirting with my bird, y' cunt?

MATTHEW smiles, taking the drink and wanders off towards JOHN.

How's he look to you?

JANINE: Your brother? I prefer you.

MARK: You know what I mean… He's different.

JANINE: You say that like it's a bad thing. Oh, blank me yeah? He's your brother. And we love him.

(Hands him empty glass.) Refill. Them kids are too quiet, man, where they at?

MARK: They're cool, babes – I've seen 'em about. Let's get you that drink…

As they approach the drinks table, they almost catch JOHN guzzling a drink. JOHN moves away hurriedly – and then realises MATTHEW has been watching him the whole time.

MATTHEW: Cool, Bruv?

JOHN: I was born cool, bruv.

MATTHEW: Listen, Johnboy… Man… I met someone who reckons he knows you.

JOHN: Where? In there? Knows me?

MATTHEW: Yeah. He gave me this. For you.

He holds out a note, which JOHN takes but does not look at.

Maybe you should give him a bell. Says you know him as Moses.

MATTHEW moves away, JOHN crumples the note and lets it fall.

SEVEN YEARS AGO – ELEPHANT & CASTLE SUPERBOWL

MATTHEW and MARK bear down on LUCY and JANINE.

MARK: Wha'appen, sista?

LUCY and JANINE look at their stalkers, expressionless.

MATTHEW: What my brother here is trying to say is what's the lick? Ain't it?

MARK: So, wha' y' saying?

JANINE and LUCY look at one another.

JANINE: What are they saying?

LUCY: I think what the brothers here're trying to say is can they buy a lady a drink.

MATTHEW: Right. So, what's a lady drinking?

LUCY kisses MATTHEW, JANINE kisses MARK. The boys reel…

White wine spritzer…

MARK: Rum and coke…

JANINE: Diet…

MARK: Y' don't need it…

LUCY and JANINE smile as they watch MATTHEW and MARK hurry off.

JANINE: What is it about white boys?

NOW – ROCKINGHAM ESTATE

LUKE, on his mobile, presses call…

LIGHTS UP on FRANKIE's home.

FRANKIE: Bermondsey Lenny?

LUKE: Bet you thought I weren't calling you back.

FRANKIE: Nah, I knew you were gonna call.

LUKE: Oh yeah? Got that desperate tone, have I?

FRANKIE: Sometimes you can just tell.

LUKE: You're right about that. I liked your ad on the dateline.
    I liked what you had to say.

FRANKIE: It's so hard to describe yourself in sixty seconds. I
    recorded my message like twelve times.

LUKE: Done mine first go.

FRANKIE: Slick.

LUKE: You inspired me.

FRANKIE: *(Laughing.)* Blimey – beyond slick.

LUKE: And honest. So – whereabouts d'y'live? Bet you're a
    Chelsea girl.

FRANKIE: Me? Leave it out!

LUKE: Leggy Sloane Ranger rich bitch slumming with a tasty
    bit of rough?

FRANKIE: Please! I'm more South London than you, mate.

LUKE: No one's more South London than me, doll. Anyway,
    my yard's north of the river these days.

FRANKIE: Oh yeah? Hampstead, are we?

LUKE: Nah. Shadwell.

FRANKIE: So only just north, then.

LUKE: Riverside loft.

FRANKIE: Nice.

LUKE: We like it. You?

FRANKIE: Tooley Street.

LUKE: Only just south, then.

FRANKIE: South enough.

LUKE: I'll tell you what – that is well fortuitous – 'cause I'm down the Elephant and Castle now.

FRANKIE: Well what?

LUKE: Fortuitous. Serendipitous. Blessed.

FRANKIE: Oh yeah? How so?

LUKE: I happen to have half-hour – how about I shoot over in me Merc and we swing by the Oxo Tower for a cocktail and a meet and greet?

FRANKIE: Now?

LUKE: Now is all we have, babe. Wassamatter – ain't got your face on?

FRANKIE: I've always got my face on.

LUKE: Sorted – what's your address?

Don't think babe – just jump – I'll catch you, babe. I'm the one – couldn't you hear it in me voice? I could hear it in yours. Sometimes you just know.

FRANKIE: I'll text it you.

LUKE: That's my girl! I'm there, yeah?

My real name's Luke – what's yours?

FRANKIE: James.

LUKE: Nah, babe, your real name…

FRANKIE: Frankie…

LUKE: Frankie. Nice. Hello Frankie.

FRANKIE: Hello Luke.

LUKE: Don't worry, Frankie. I'll catch you.

He hangs up…

BRIDIE approaches MARK.

BRIDIE: You think your brother's alright?

MARK: Which one?

BRIDIE: They all try to be clever with me – like I'm not the one what made them that way.

MARK: He's fine.

BRIDIE: And they all try to lie to me like I'm not the one what taught 'em to lie. Like I'm not a mind-reading witch.

MARK: Like you're not the Uber-mother.

BRIDIE: Is there any other kind of mother? I could learn a thing or two from your Janine, though. One look at them kids and it's like the bleedin' *Matrix*. They just freeze in mid-air.

MARK: Yeah, she's good…

BRIDIE: You hold onto that one, she's a diamond. Reminds me of me.

JOHN: I notice no one from his team bothered coming down.

MARK: Midweek match tomorrow. Can't be around booze, can they?

BRIDIE: Bollocks. He's given that team his life and they've barely let him play.

JOHN: Tossers.

BRIDIE: Bastards. I've told him have a word with your agent and go where you're bleedin' appreciated.

JOHN: 'cept his agent ain't turned up.

BRIDIE: I tell you son, the whole world's just a bunch of cunts. That's why you should try and be a bit more decent-er to that poor girl.

JOHN: Mum…

BRIDIE: That girl's the most decent one you've got between you.

MARK: Mum leave it.

BRIDIE: I'm leaving it.

Pause.

They go silent.

So what you gonna do about the baby?

JOHN: Baby?

BRIDIE: Dincha know? I'm with child.

(Rolls her eyes, smokes.) Have you even looked at your girlfriend lately? She's teeming with it – like a thingy dish.

MARK: Petri.

BRIDIE: Yeah, one o' them. Teeming…

(Smokes.) …with life.

JOHN: She ain't my girlfriend.

BRIDIE: Let's hope it ain't your baby, then.

EIGHT MONTHS AGO – BEDROOM

SUNAI sleeps. JOHN watches her. He picks up the Koran – he looks at it and smiles. Opens it near the beginning. Reads…

JOHN: *'Does there not pass over a man a space of time when his life is a blank?'*

> *(Turning back a page.)* *'When the sky is rent asunder, when the stars scatter and the oceans roll together; when the graves are hurled about; each soul shall know what it has done…*
>
> *(Pause.) and what it has…*
>
> *(Looking at SUNAI.) …failed to do…'*
>
> *The door opens and LUKE comes in.*

LUKE: Alright, man?

> *JOHN puts his finger to his lips.*
>
> Sorry, bruv.
>
> *He walks quietly forward a bit.*
>
> Is that her, then?
>
> *(Peering over at her.)* Big night yeah? She's alright, y'knowdat?
>
> *(Seeing JOHN's face.)* Later, yeah? Sweet.
>
> *He leaves. JOHN continues to read. Sleepily SUNAI reaches out and touches JOHN's face. He shrugs her away – then shifts himself to sit out of her reach… He reads…*

JOHN: *'Unclean women…are for unclean men.'*

NOW – ROCKINGHAM ESTATE

LUKE approaches MARK.

LUKE: Mark, lend us your car keys back, yeah?

MARK: Where you going now in the middle of your brother's party, y'snidey bastard?

LUKE: I gotta make a quick dash – no one'll know I'm gone.

MARK: Girl trouble?

LUKE: No such thing as girl trouble, mate – just blokes who can't handle 'em.

MARK: Well you can go after Mattman meets the press, alright?

MATTHEW: Go where, man?

LUKE: Nowhere bruv – quick run over to Tooley Street.

MATTHEW: Hot date, bruv?

LUKE: Ain't easy being me.

MATTHEW: Couldn't give us a lift, could you?

MARK: Where the fuck are you going? You ain't trying to tell me no one'll notice you're fucking gone! You're going over Lucy's, ain't you? I'll drive you after the press 'ting.

LUKE: Man, we can't all go!

MARK: You want my car – you drive us over Lucy's – and then you go and pick up what you got to pick up and then come back and get us, yeah?

LUKE: Do what?

MARK: You fucking heard. Let's do it, Mattman.

THE PRESS rushes MATTHEW.

PRESS: Matt! Matt! Over here! Matt!

They hold out a clutch of dictaphones.

PRESS ONE: Matt, you're back.

MATTHEW: Thanks for telling us, mate – I was confused there a moment.

PRESS TWO: So how's it been in the hospital?

MATTHEW: Hospitable.

PRESS THREE: How were the fellow inmates?

MATTHEW: Matey.

PRESS THREE: …I mean at football?

MATTHEW: Oh! Football! What's football?

PRESS FOUR: So you haven't played for the last year?

MATTHEW: Has it really been a year? Time flies when you're having shock therapy.

PRESS FIVE: What do you say to those who reckon you only sectioned yourself to get out of being drug-tested?

MATTHEW: Drug-tested? What are they on? I have nothing to hide 'cept my trackmarks.

PRESS SIX: And are you hoping to return to Millwall?

PRESS TWO: Any truth to the rumours that you're thinking of going abroad?

MATTHEW: I prefer the one that I'm becoming a broad – that's my favourite.

MARK: Last question, yeah, lads?

PRESS ONE: Matt! We all remember when you scored your one goal for the first team –

MATTHEW: Didn't know you cared, mate.

PRESS ONE: …but what most people really remember is your tearful dedication of that goal to your dad… Wishing he was there to say 'Good on you, son'… What do you think he'd say to you today?

MATTHEW: He'd probably say 'Your round, son – mine's a pint.' Then he'd kick the shit out of me.

There is uncertain laughter.

Then he'd probably make me suck his dick. Then he might fuck me up the arse. Then he'd make me say thank you. And we'd go back to training.

(Pause.) Any more questions?

Silence.

Thank you.

Silence. MARK laughs.

MARK: Matthew Fucking Prospect! You fucked-up funny bastard. Okay, people – party's over.

No one moves…

I said, fuck off the lot of ya! Party's fucking over! What the fuck are you looking at, y'cunt? Alright – I'm gonna count to three… One…two…

LIGHT CHANGE

MARK: …three.

A SHORT WHILE LATER

MATTHEW, MARK, LUKE and JOHN, BRIDIE and JANINE in silence.

BRIDIE: Better put the food in the freezer.

JANINE: I'll help you, Bride, yeah?

BRIDIE: You already done the cooking, love, that's enough…

MARK: No, Mum, you're alright.

BRIDIE: No, son, *you're* alright. You know I like things how
    I like 'em – You'll only fuck it up. Just look after your
    brother, yeah?

    She hurries off.

MARK: What the fuck did you have to say that for, bruv?

MATTHEW: 'Cause it was true.

JOHN: They doing truth this week down the institution, then?

LUKE: Bruv…

JOHN: Well, what's he fucking want? A tin medal?

LUKE: Mum'll be alright, Mattman.

JOHN: Yeah, she can just pretend nothing's happened. She's
    good at that.

JANINE: I'll take the kids home…

MARK: Need the motor? Oh, no you…

JANINE: I've got mine…

MARK: Got yours…

JANINE: Okay then.

    *She gives him a kiss. Then as she leaves she stops to kiss BRIDIE,
    before hurrying off, calling the kids…*

    (To kids.) You lot..!

TEN YEARS AGO – FRONT ROOM

SOUND FX: Televised footie match. LUKE and JOHN quietly approaching sleeping DAD – whose face we cannot see.

LUKE: Shhhh!

JOHN: Chill, man – 'kin siren won't wake him…

> *LUKE picks up remote control – turns down the TV – DAD's breathing fills the room…*

JOHN: Earthquake – volcano – fucking world war three…

…ain't nothing gonna wake him!

LUKE: Will you shut the fuck up? It ain't about waking him – s'bout you getting on my fuckin' wick!

JOHN: *(Ear-splitting.)* DAD!

> *DAD does not stir.*

Y'see?

> *BRIDIE's voice from off.*

BRIDIE: YOU LOT!

LUKE: *(Swiping JOHN.)* Y'cunt! What Mum?

BRIDIE: What you doing down there?

LUKE: Watching telly!

BRIDIE: Bollocks are ya! Leave your dad alone!

JOHN: Mum, shush! Dad's tryin'a sleep!

BRIDIE: Cheeky little fucker – I'll swing for you – go out the house and make your mischief – you're cracking my fucking face-pack!

LUKE/JOHN: Alright, Mum!

BRIDIE: I mean it!

> *JOHN and LUKE start pulling objects from their dad's pockets.*

LUKE: …Tobacco….

JOHN: …Rizlas…

LUKE: …betting slip…

JOHN: …Greasy comb…

LUKE: Vain baldy bastard…

…Lottery ticket…

JOHN: Snotrag – urr! Fuckin' hell, man, can't he get a fucking wallet?

LUKE: *(Finding something.)* Ah!

JOHN: What?

LUKE: Tenner.

JOHN: Yes!

LUKE: No notes!

JOHN: *(Grabbing at it.)* Fuck that!

LUKE: *(Keeping it out of reach.)* Fuck off!

JOHN: Luke, man!

LUKE: He notices notes!

JOHN: He don't notice if his dick's hanging out after a slash! Alright. Cool…

JOHN: Wicked!

LUKE: But if we get caught you take the blame, yeah?

JOHN: You what, y'cunt?

LUKE: Mum'll protect you!

JOHN: Bollocks! I ain't admitting I jacked Dad, he'll slaughter me!

LUKE: Don't admit, it – Deny it, y' thick fucker! Deny it. But act guilty – he'll go for you – Mum'll protect her little favourite – sorted!

JOHN: Deal!

LUKE: Swear on Mum's life?

JOHN: I can't swear on Mum's life – I'll swear on Dad's life.

LUKE: Yeah, 'cause it ain't worth nothing.

JOHN: Mine then! I swear on my name as a Prospect – on a Prospect boy's word of honour.

LUKE: Cool.

JOHN: But we split it six to me, three to you – yeah?

LUKE: Stroll on! Who's older?

JOHN: Who's taking the blame?

LUKE: Who found it?

JOHN: Who didn't want it?

LUKE: And who's got it?

JOHN: Fucking tea leaf.

They start putting the stuff back in DAD's pockets.

I'm gonna score me some weed, yeah?

(Indicating foot-long joint.) You can get spliffs this big. I'm connected. Serious, yeah, what you spending yours on?

LUKE: Bird.

JOHN: Bird? Fuckin' cock'a'two, you mean.

LUKE looks at JOHN with no expression.

(Quick.) Joke!

LUKE reaches over his dad – grabs his brother's face…

Mum!

LUKE plants a great big kiss on him.

Y'bent cunt!

At that moment – DAD coughs – spraying both boys' faces with blood. They stare a moment, stunned.

LUKE & JOHN: Muuuuum!

TEN YEARS AGO – BEDROOM

MATTHEW is pacing up and down, MARK hurries in with a bowl of water and flannel.

MARK: Okay, okay, okay, here we go…

MATTHEW: Markman! Where the fuck…?

MARK: Okay, bruv, I'm sorry. I'm here…

MARK places the bowl of water on the ground, ringing out the flannel.

…okay, here we go…

MARK looks at MATTHEW – who is staring at the ground.

(Gently.) Here we go, Bruv.

MATTHEW pulls up his shirt – his body is covered in bruises.

Fuck bruv!

MATTHEW drops his shirt.

It's okay, bruv…

MARK reaches out, lifts his brother's shirt and dabs at a wound on his back.

'Zat too hot?

MATTHEW: It's fine.

MARK: You sure?

MATTHEW: It's fine.

MARK: I fucking hate Dad.

MATTHEW: Don't say that, man.

MARK: Well, he hates us!

MATTHEW: It ain't us. It's that penalty.

MARK: Do what?

MATTHEW: That penalty, yesterday. I shouldn't have missed it.

MARK: Is that what this lot was for? You miss a penalty and he batters you? You fucking scored twice!

MATTHEW: You should never miss. He's right about that. He was just coaching me. Warrior style.

MARK: Warrior?

MATTHEW: You take the penalty – If it goes wide you don't cry about it – you lay down and you take your licks.

MARK: He kicked the shit out of you.

MATTHEW: First thing this morning – penalty training – an hundred penalty kicks – twenty went wide – But only in the first seventy-four. Last twenty-six was clean in. Warrior style – Samurai.

MARK: I'd like to kill him.

MATTHEW: Markman…

MARK: If I could get away with it, I would.

MATTHEW: You don't know what you're saying.

MARK: I fucking do. I ain't the big brother, mate, I don't have to be all responsible. He's a cunt.

MATTHEW: Leave it out, Mark. He's our dad.

MARK: One day we'll be grown up and we'll be taller than him and you'll be a football fucking superstar and Mum'll realise she don't love him and live with one of us and he'll be alone. And he'll say – 'I'm your dad.' And I'll get right in his face and say, calm and cool – 'You're a cunt.' And I can't fucking wait.

From upstairs they hear..

JOHN/LUKE: Muuuuuuuuuuum!

TEN YEARS AGO – LIVING ROOM

BRIDIE rushes in to find the two boys looking at their dead DAD. She looks for a long moment…

BRIDIE: Luke – call an ambulance and the old bill – in that order – John – fetch your brothers.

No one moves.

(*Quietly.*) Now, please.

LUKE leaves first. JOHN follows a moment after. BRIDIE approaches DAD. Kneels in front of him, searches his face.

You silly old sod.

MATTHEW and MARK arrive with JOHN – they stop in the doorway, breathless.

MATTHEW: Mum?

BRIDIE: Matthew… It's down to you now.

She leaves MATTHEW, MARK and JOHN staring at their dead father. LUKE arrives.

MATTHEW: We should close his eyes.

No one moves. MARK bursts into tears. LUKE reaches out to touch him.

LUKE: Markman..!

MARK: Cunt fucking got away with it!

TEN YEARS AGO – CHAPEL OF REST

MATTHEW, MARK, LUKE and JOHN looking down at their dead father.

MARK: Fucking Hell, man… He's shrunk.

LUKE: It ain't him. He ain't there.

MARK: Let's fucking face it – he never really was.

JOHN: What's that in his mouth?

JOHN reaches in to the casket.

MARK: Is he wearing make-up? Fuck, don't touch him, y'cunt!

JOHN: They've stitched his mouth up!

MARK: Thank fuck for that – stop playing with him – he ain't a fucking Action Man!

JOHN: He n'arf cold.

MARK: Er, that's 'cause he's dead.

JOHN: Yeah, but it's weird – I've never touched someone who's cold from the inside.

MARK: That's 'cause you never tried touching him when he was alive.

LUKE: Where do you think he's gone?

MARK: He was a fucking witch's tit.

LUKE: He must have gone somewhere, mustn't he? Maybe he's finally decided to go further than the pub and see what's out there.

MARK: What the fuck are you on about? You can see where the fuck he is.

LUKE: And this is what he's left behind? This shrunk-up white shred? All them pints, all them early mornings on demolition, all them late nights on the piss, greasy dinners, fivers on the gee-gees, Saturdays down the dogs, all them farts and smelly socks. Forty-four years what's he left to show for it?

MATTHEW: Us.

(Pause.) We're what he's left. This. Us.

(Pause) We're it.

Long pause.

JOHN: I wonder if there's anything in his pockets?

TEN YEARS AGO – CHURCH

MATTHEW steps up.

MATTHEW: When Eamonn Patrick Prospect come over to England as a kid – There were all the signs in landlords' windows – 'No dogs, no blacks, no Irish.' Teachers used to rip the piss out of his accent, then wink and say, 'Just taking the Mick'. Kids used to chuck potatoes at him at dinner-time, and when the caretaker spat in his face once with no warning. The whole school cheered. When he spat back the headmaster suspended him. Dad waited for him after school with a bunch of keys in a sock – he got him in the back of the head. Never got caught. Never went back to school. He hated dogs for the rest of his life, and blacks – and just to be fair he hated the Irish worst of all. 'Cause Dad was a cunt. Everybody here knew him, yeah? Worked with him, drank with him, was related to him, met him. Then you know. Dad was a cunt. And now he's dead. And it's time for me to step up and be a man. How the fuck do I do that? We never got round to that little chat. I suppose I'm supposed to forgive him. And suppose what I'm supposed to do today is ask you lot to forgive him too. It'll take you a while. But what the hell, think about it, yeah? I will. Tell you what – next time we're all together – next wedding, christening, funeral – whoever's forgiven him by then…speak up, yeah? …Cool.

MATTHEW steps down.

TEN YEARS AGO – ROCKINGHAM ESTATE

MATTHEW dribbles the ball through his brothers. They get nowhere near it…

LUKE: Shit!

MARK: Fuck!

JOHN: Bastard!

MATTHEW juggles the ball with his feet with determination.
Bru-uvv!

MARK: 'Fuck sake, bruv, let some other cunt have the fucker!

LUKE, who's been weighing things up, nips in to get the ball.

LUKE: Yeaaahhhhh!

MARK & JOHN: Yeaaaaahhhhh!

MATTHEW cuts straight back in with a crippling tackle.

LUKE: Aah, shit, man!

MATTHEW: *(Juggling with his feet.)* Sorry, bruv!

LUKE: *(Limping in circles.)* I'm fine, bruv!

JOHN: I ain't playing with that cunt, he's lethal!

BRIDIE: You lot! Dinner!

JOHN: Thank fuck for that!

    (Heading in.) Mum, I'm vegan, now!

MARK: Mattman! It's only a bleedin' game! You alright, Luke?

    LUKE has rolled down his sock to check out a deep gouge.

LUKE: Flea bite, man – looks good, though don't it?

    BRIDIE comes out of the house…

BRIDIE: You lot deaf, stupid or taking the piss?

MARK: Just helping Luke, Mum…

BRIDIE: Good luck, darlin'.

LUKE: *(Shrugging MARK away.)* I'm sweet, bruv, leave it.

BRIDIE: What the fuck's wrong with you?

LUKE: Nothing's wrong with me…

BRIDIE: I wish…

    MARK and LUKE go in. BRIDIE watches MATTHEW still juggling.

    We're gonna be alright, son.

MATTHEW: Too right we are, Mum.

BRIDIE: They'll accept you in Millwall.

MATTHEW: I know.

BRIDIE: They will.

MATTHEW: I know.

    BRIDIE watches him a moment longer – then goes in. MATTHEW keeps playing…

TEN YEARS AGO – LUKE AND JOHN'S BEDROOM

MATTHEW reads a book that LUKE is holding for him.

LUKE: Yeah…?

MATTHEW: *'It was…because…I heard…father and mother,'* he… *explained…*

LUKE: Good…

MATTHEW: *…in a low…voice, talking about what I was to be when I…became a man.' He was extra –* what the fuck?

LUKE: *'…Extraordinarily…'*

MATTHEW: Why can't he just say very?

He was very… What's that?

LUKE: *Agitated.*

MATTHEW: Supposed to be a fucking kids' book! *He was*

(Dismissively from memory.) extraordinarily agitated now. 'I don't want ever to be a man, he said with…

LUKE: *…passion…*

MATTHEW: *(Quick.) …Passion, I want always to be a little boy and have fun'* – Deal with it mate – *'So I ran away to Ken…*

LUKE: *…sington gardens…*

MATTHEW: *…and lived a long time among the fairies.'* Man, what the fuck are we reading? No wonder I can't get it – them words ain't meant to come out of a Geezer's mouth, mate!

LUKE: It's just *Peter Pan*, bruv.

MATTHEW: What's the big deal about reading anyfuckingway? I've got this fucking far, ain't I? I'm fucking going into the first fucking division, mate. How stupid is that?

LUKE: No one thinks you're stupid, Mattman.

MATTHEW: 'Cause no one knows I can't read.

LUKE: 'Cause no one cares.

MATTHEW: 'Cause I got legs.

(Grabs the book – reads.) 'I ran away the day I was born'

LUKE: Excellent, bruv.

MATTHEW: *She gave him a look of the most in…*

LUKE: *Intense…*

MATTHEW: I know! *Intense… Ad… ad…*

LUKE: *Admiration.*

MATTHEW hurls the book away.

MATTHEW: FUCK IT! …Fuck it.

TEN YEARS AGO – OXO TOWER

LUKE sits alone at the table. He is looking at the menu. BRIDIE approaches.

BRIDIE: Fucking hell, that bog was a trial.

> *LUKE pulls out the chair for her.*

> There's some old bird sat there hiding behind the door what jumps out and sprays you with perfume – scaring the crap out of you…

LUKE: You can sit, Mum.

BRIDIE: *(Sits.)* …And then she hands you loo roll and stands there with her hand out. Now that's just creepy.

LUKE: Menu, Mum.

BRIDIE: *(Picks up menu.)* Tipping in the lav – what's that about? For what? Ain't like I couldn't do it on me own… Fucking Ada, look at these prices.

LUKE: Don't worry about it, Mum – 'scuse! Er, waiter!

WAITER: Sir.

LUKE: Could we have, er… Some wine?

WAITER: House wine? Red or white?

BRIDIE: Red.

LUKE: What's house wine?

WAITER: That's our own label.

BRIDIE: Like Tesco's own brand down the supermarket.

LUKE: Nah, fuck that. Something nice.

BRIDIE: *(To WAITER.)* What's nice, darlin'?

WAITER: Nice?

LUKE: What would you have that you couldn't afford normally, if you could afford it.

WAITER: *(Points.)* The Châteauneuf-du-Pape '95…?

LUKE: Bottle of that, yeah? Safe.

> *The WAITER goes away.*

BRIDIE: They gonna let you drink as well?

LUKE: 'Course they are.

BRIDIE: You're not even thirteen.

LUKE: This is a cool place Mum. Relax.

BRIDIE: Listen to you – have you been here before?

LUKE: I've seen it on telly.

BRIDIE: Listen to it. He's mental. How can you afford this? No, don't tell me, I don't wanna know…

LUKE: It's cool, Mum.

BRIDIE: It's better if you don't tell me where you got it…

LUKE: I won it Mum.

BRIDIE: Gambling at your age…

LUKE: I ain't been gambling. I won it on the lottery.

BRIDIE: Oh. Well then. How much?

LUKE: Two hundred and eighty.

BRIDIE: *(Impressed.)* Two hundred and eighty. And you spent it on this.

LUKE: On you. And them flowers for Dad. I wanted to take you somewhere. I've wanted to see you smile for a long time. I know you wish Dad was here. So do I. I wish he'd brung you here hisself. Bought you that dress.

BRIDIE: He'd have hated it here.

LUKE: He'd have loved hating it though.

(Examining her.) Whoops! Half a smile! Watch it – you'll spoil me.

BRIDIE: You are an odd little sod. You take after me.

(Looking out the window.) I used to be all secrets myself once – all dreams and schemes…

WAITER pours puzzled LUKE a taster.

LUKE: Hey, mate – wassatabout?

BRIDIE tastes it for him.

BRIDIE: …ta, love…

(Drinking and gazing out the window.) I s'pose this view is worth something. Is that St Paul's…?

The WAITER pours LUKE and BRIDIE's wine…

LUKE: Ta, mate…

BRIDIE: …Where Diana got married…

LUKE: …Pour one for yourself, yeah…?

BRIDIE: …Poor little bitch.

LUKE: See that light on over there? That gaff with the high ceilings? That's a flat, Mum. They call 'em lofts.

BRIDIE: All that money and no net curtains. That's what you call a yuppie slum. One good thing about being south of the river. You get the view. What are they looking at? Council flats and crap.

LUKE: And you and me…

BRIDIE: …getting pissed….

BRIDIE smiles…

EIGHT YEARS AGO – FRONT ROOM

The phone is ringing. BRIDIE, MARK, LUKE and JOHN gather as MATTHEW, ball under his arm, hurries in to answer it. They stand round him, drinking in every word.

MATTHEW: Yeah? Yeah, guvnor, speaking… Yeah. No probs…

(Covers the receiver.) I'm on hold. Busy man.

Everyone waits.

MARK: You know what? This feels good.

Man's gonna get *paid*, Geeze! Gonna get *paper!*

MATTHEW: And Mum's gonna get one of them whassits Lukey showed her –

BRIDIE/LUKE: – Lofts –

MATTHEW: Lofts. Only you're gonna have fucking curtains.

(Uncovering receiver.) Yeah…

(Listens, expressionless.) Excellent.

The FAMILY ripples with a suppressed excitement.

Yeah, yeah. Brilliant.

(Pause.) Thanks guv.

MATTHEW hangs up. All eyes on him.

BRIDIE: What position?

MATTHEW: Striker.

More excitement.

Reserve team.

Long silence.

LUKE: Bruv – that's brilliant.

MARK: First reserve. Millwall.

JOHN: That's the fucking business.

Pause. LUKE steps forwards offers a fist…

LUKE: I'm proud of you, bruv.

LUKE and MATTHEW touch fists.

LUKE leaves.

JOHN: Wait 'til I tell them lot in school, man… First reserve!

JOHN leaves.

MARK: Celebrate tonight, yeah? Get rat-arsed!

MATTHEW: Cool.

MARK: Give it a year you'll be running the gaff, Geeze.

MARK leaves.

We are the Prospects,
Beautiful Prospects…

BRIDIE looks at MATTHEW.

MATTHEW: You will get your house, Mum.

BRIDIE: Don't talk daft…

MATTHEW: You will. I ain't Dad, Mum.

BRIDIE: I ain't your Dad, neither, son. I know you won't let me down.

She leaves.

MATTHEW drops the ball to his feet, starts to juggle – he fumbles it. Stops – stares at the ground, trying to control his breathing…

MATTHEW leaves – the ball rolls aimlessly centre stage…

TEN YEARS AGO – BEDROOM

MATTHEW and LUKE sit side by side. LUKE is eating from a tube of Pringles. MATTHEW's arm round LUKE's shoulders.

MATTHEW: You keep your eyes on the screen, yeah? You do not look round. You know she's relaxing when you hear the popcorn crunching coming nearer…

LUKE is letting his head slowly fall sideways to rest on MATTHEW's shoulder.

Remain breathing normally. Until you get contact… Then you relax the arm that's round her shoulder until your hand is limp…

(Doing all this.) …until your thumb…ever so gently…grazes her nipple…if she keeps eating…you're in.

LUKE eats another Pringle.

LUKE: Then what?

MATTHEW: That's when you reach across with your hand… hold it open…and you wait 'til she gives you some popcorn…

LUKE: What if she don't give you none?

MATTHEW: Then you better have chose a fucking good film or else you're wasting your time.

LUKE puts some Pringles in MATTHEW's open hand.

But if she gives you some, then you're in, 'cause the next thing you do is you let it drop.

(The Pringle falls into his own lap.) And you leave it there until she notices – and when she does… And she will…

MATTHEW opens his legs slightly…

You wait…

LUKE reaches into MATTHEW's lap for the Pringle. MATTHEW reaches out and puts his hand on LUKE's and holds it there.

LUKE: *(Laughs.)* Sick, man!

LUKE tries to take his hand away – MATTHEW holds it there.

Okay, Mattman.

MATTHEW: It's cool, Lukeman…

LUKE: *(Trying harder.)* Man, it's okay!

MATTHEW: *(Holding.)* I don't mind…

LUKE: Stop it, Dad!

MATTHEW yanks his hand away. Pringles explode everywhere. He thinks for a moment. He gets up abruptly and leaves.

NOW – LUCY'S DOOR

MARK watches as MATTHEW, holding a rose, produces a key – thinks better of it – puts it away. He speaks to the locked door.

MATTHEW: Lucy! Lucy, you know I had to come. You know I can't stay. I don't want to desert you again or scare you again. But I just had to say hello and goodbye and sorry Lucy. I'm sorry, Lucy.

The door opens – and there is LUCY. She looks at him

LUCY: *(Gently.)* Hello… Goodbye.

NOW – FRANKIE'S FRONT DOOR

LUKE checks himself out before knocking. FRANKIE opens the door.

FRANKIE: Oh my God.

LUKE: Oh *my* God.

FRANKIE: You're so young.

LUKE: So are you – Oh, there you go.

LUKE offers her a rose.

FRANKIE: You're so handsome. I'm sorry.

She closes the door. LUKE knocks again.

LUKE: Oy, Frankie. I ain't so young, trust me darlin', I've seen things. And I ain't as handsome as I look. And now I come all the way from the Elephant to take you out and you slam the door on me and break my heart. I thought you was a lady, Frankie – Be a lady, yeah – don't break my heart.

Pause. FRANKIE opens the door. LUKE smiles.

TEN YEARS AGO – MATTHEW & MARK'S BEDROOM

MATTHEW in bed in the dark. There is a knock at the door. No reaction. LUKE comes in.

LUKE: Bruv?

> *He sits on the side of the bed.*
>
> I'm sorry, bruv.
>
> *(Pause.)* I don't mind you touching me bruv. I don't mind if it's you… Bruv?
>
> *LUKE reaches out and takes MATTHEW's shaking hand.*
>
> It's okay, Mattman… I want you to.
>
> *He places the hand in his lap.*
>
> Teach me, bruv… Teach me.

> *Interval.*

SEVEN YEARS AGO – CATS WHISKERS CLUB

MATTHEW and LUCY, JANINE and MARK slow-dancing. JANINE reaches out and taps MATTHEW's shoulder…

JANINE: Oy! Legs!

MATTHEW: Oy! Lungs!

JANINE: Your brother reckons you're a bit of a Beckham!

MATTHEW: You should see me in a sarong, doll!

> *(Smiles at LUCY.)* So where'd'ya get a name like Lucy?

LUCY: I left a note for Santa.

MATTHEW: Well, I like what he left in your stockings…

LUCY: Yeah, yeah, whatever…

JANINE: So, what do you do? Wide-boy?

MARK: I *know* you ain't calling me a white boy…

JANINE: Wide-boy, darlin'. Wi-i-D-e boy… Wow, that rocked your world! Is being a white boy so bad?

MARK: I wouldn't know, innit?

JANINE: …Don't tell me – you feel black.

MARK: I ain't white, I know that much.

JANINE: So you're a brother is it?

MARK: And you're a sista innit?

JANINE: Actually we are sisters. That's my babygirl right there…

MARK: And sistas and brothers make a family, don't it?

JANINE: You know it. So you never been out with a white bird?

MARK: What can I say? I aim high.

JANINE: And once in a while, you score…

LUCY: Play the beautiful game do you?

MATTHEW: Been known to kick a ball about.

MARK: Yeah, only for fucking Millwall.

LUCY: Oh, I've heard of them.

MARK: Oh, she's heard of 'em. He's a first reserve, babe – He's the man.

LUCY: I noticed. What position?

MATTHEW: You what?

LUCY: …do you play? Don't tell me – forward. Nothing reserved about you.

MATTHEW: Do you always talk in word games?

LUCY: …too easily bored, that's my trouble. What's yours?

MATTHEW: Used to be everything – Now it's just you.

LUCY: Then you're fucked, darlin'…

> *Kisses him.*

MATTHEW: Fine by me.

NOW – OUTSIDE LUCY'S

LUCY: Where are you going?

MATTHEW: I dunno. Somewhere I s'pose. I've never really been anywhere. Be free maybe – like you always said.

LUCY: Yeah.

MATTHEW: I don't suppose you're available?

LUCY: To be free?

MATTHEW: Just thought I'd ask.

LUCY: Some people just can't be together.

MATTHEW: I know. But I had to come here anyway. So you could send me away. To confirm that this is broken. One of them fucked-up tragic stories where they both thought about each other, but never saw each other again. And here's the part where you watch me walk away. I look back and the door is closed.

LUCY: We don't kiss, We don't even say another word.

MATTHEW: We just wear each other like scars for the rest of our lives.

MARK watches as MATTHEW looks at her and walks away…then turns to catch the door closing. MATTHEW continues leaving, MARK pursues.

MARK: Bruv!

MATTHEW: Bruv.

MARK: Bruv, she still wants you! You fucking had her *there*, man. And you're fucking walking away.

MATTHEW: Some people just can't be together, mate.

MARK: Don't give me that riddle-me-this shit. Are you gonna fucking talk to me or what? Where you going?

MATTHEW: I wanna run.

MARK: You don't want me to come with you.

MATTHEW: I'll see you back home.

MARK: Why'd you go to Johnboy?

MATTHEW: Johnboy?

MARK: When you lost the plot. Why'd you call him? He was the youngest – We were closer – but you called him.

MATTHEW: S'pose I thought he'd understand, mate. He's never felt comfortable in his skin neither.

MARK: And I have? Fucking look at me. I can't even fucking be still.

MATTHEW: I know, Geeze. You're a black lesbian woman. I know that.

MARK: What? Y'don't have to fucking overdo it, mate…

MATTHEW: You're black trapped in white, you're her trapped in him. More than all of us, I can see it now. Finally. Sorry bruv. I should've called you.

MARK: Fucking hell, Mattman. Go on, You run, y'cunt, don't make me come with you and show you up again.

MATTHEW: Laters.

MARK: Laters.

MATTHEW starts to run.

TEN YEARS AGO – MATTHEW & MARK'S BEDROOM

MATTHEW and MARK in their separate beds.

MARK: Bruv?

MATTHEW: Bruv?

MARK: You sleeping?

MATTHEW: No. Why, are you?

MARK: I saw you, man.

MATTHEW: Go to sleep, bruv.

MARK: You and Luke.

MATTHEW: I've got training in the morning.

Pause.

MARK: You used to do that with Dad, dincha?

Pause.

MATTHEW: Yeah.

MARK: I used to hear him with you. And with Luke sometimes.

MATTHEW: Go to sleep.

MARK: Mattman…

MATTHEW: Go to sleep.

MARK: Does it hurt?

MATTHEW: Depends.

MARK: Matt, bruv.

MATTHEW: Sleep, bruv.

MARK: Is there something wrong with me? Ain't I worth hurting?

MATTHEW: Count yourself lucky, mate,

MARK: Yeah, that's me – lucky. Will you show us? Bruv?

MARK gets up.

Bruv?

He approaches his brother's bed…

Bruv?

He gets into MATTHEW's bed.

Bruv?

MARK lies with his back to MATTHEW…

Bruv?

MATTHEW slips his arm round MARK…

MATTHEW: Shhhh…

TWO YEARS AGO – MATTHEW & LUCY'S FLAT.

LUCY is asleep on the sofa. MATTHEW staggers in. He sits beside her and looks down at her – he blows gently on her face. She opens her eyes.

LUCY: Mmmm… Hello, superstar.

MATTHEW: You left the TV on.

LUCY: I was watching you.

MATTHEW: You saw it?

LUCY: Of course I saw it. I watch every match – just in case. Did you know you were going on tonight?

MATTHEW: I was praying…

(Grins.) And they were answered!

He throws his arms around her and whoops.

LUCY: You were brilliant! Brilliant!

MATTHEW: I was pretty fucking brilliant weren't I?

LUCY: That far off being man of the match…

MATTHEW: Say that again…

LUCY: …they got to pull you into the first team after that – Say what?

MATTHEW: 'Man of…'?

LUCY: Man of the match…

They kiss. His phone rings.

MATTHEW: Shit.

He pulls the phone out his pocket and answers.

What you want, y' cunt?

MARK: A goal, y' cunt!

MATTHEW: Fuck off, y' cunt!

MARK: Learn to play, y' cunt!

MATTHEW: Hanging up, y' cunt!

MARK: Proud o' ya, y' cunt!

MATTHEW/MARK: Laters.

They hang up. MATTHEW throws the phone aside and turns back to LUCY.

LUCY: You're funny.

MATTHEW: I am thankful madam finds me amusing…

LUCY: …every other word is cunt.

MATTHEW: Cunt on the brain, that's me.

LUCY: 'Cept you never call it that.

MATTHEW: Come again?

LUCY: Your coach is a cunt, your teachers were cunts, bad drivers are cunts – your brothers are cunts…

MATTHEW: Such language for a young lady…

LUCY: Everything's a cunt except the one thing that is. Interesting.

MATTHEW: What you got ain't a cunt, darlin'.

LUCY: *(Laughs.)* What is it, then?

MATTHEW: It's a pussy, innit? Soft and strokable – with a mind of its own. The c-word's too cruel sounding – Listen to it – Ker-Unt! It's too much like 'cock'…hard. Pussy is soft…like a kiss –

(Breathy.) Puhhsseee… Puhhsseee… Gets me hard everytime… You get me?

LUCY: I get you – but what about what I wanna give you? I want us to share everything. Uncensored. Explicit. Open. Honest. And the honest truth is – it ain't just strokable, darlin' – it's complicated down there. It's a catacomb – it's canals and clenches and a clit…it's Cuntville – 'Y'all come back now!'

MATTHEW: Can't she be a cunt to someone else?

(Sighs, lowering his head to LUCY's lap.) Sorry, cunty…I accept your cuntiness in all its cuntilicious glory.

Clambering onto MATTHEW, LUCY wraps her legs round him.

LUCY: Tell me something you've never told anyone. Say something you've never said out loud.

MATTHEW: I used to fuck my brothers.

…All of 'em.

LUCY: You naughty boys. Who was the best kisser? Bet it was Luke.

MATTHEW: Lucy. You don't kiss your brother.

LUCY: Why not?

MATTHEW: Not like that. Babe, I didn't like it. I don't know why I did it. I don't know why.

LUCY: It happens. When I was thirteen I gave my uncle a blow-job for tickets to see Take That.

Just 'cause you don't like it don't mean you don't need it.

(Pause.) I can be your brother if you want…

MATTHEW: My brother?

LUCY: I can be anyone. Tell me who you want me to be… Do what you want to me…

MATTHEW: Lucy…

LUCY: …I'm only Lucy if you want me to be…when you want me to be. I want you to be free with me…be free… Matthew?

(Kissing him.) Matthew, bruv?

MATTHEW: Yes, bruv?

LUCY smiles and slowly moves in – they kiss.

NOW – THE OXO TOWER RESTAURANT

LUKE takes FRANKIE's coat, lays it over the back of the chair. He pulls out FRANKIE's chair for her to sit, then sits himself. He gazes at FRANKIE as she places her bag under the table. He hands her the menu. She tries to look at it, distracted by his staring.

FRANKIE: What?

LUKE: I'm watching your hands.

FRANKIE: Oh God!

LUKE: Do you play the piano?

FRANKIE: I wish.

LUKE: You should.

    WAITER arrives.

WAITER: Good evening.

LUKE: Getting there. Wine for the lady.

WAITER: House, sir?

LUKE: Châteauneuf-du-Pape 95 – a bottle.

WAITER: Good choice.

LUKE: I know. Thanks.

    WAITER departs.

FRANKIE: Beyond slick… So do you bring all your dates here?

LUKE: Only the special ones.

    FRANKIE stares at him a moment. They laugh.

    Straight up.

FRANKIE: And how long have you been a tranny tracker?

LUKE: A what?

FRANKIE: A tracker of trannies. One who seeks the company of the scarier sex.

LUKE: You don't have to talk about yourself like that. You don't have to laugh at yourself in case I do. Laugh at all of them out there. You ain't what's really scary.

FRANKIE: Tell that to my neighbours.

LUKE: If they're scared of you they're cowards and simpletons. Fuck 'em.

FRANKIE: No thanks.

LUKE: They been giving you shit then?

FRANKIE: Just the usual.

LUKE: Like what?

FRANKIE: Chucking bottles, breaking windows, fireworks through the letterbox. Nothing original. I'm too busy getting on with it to really notice.

LUKE: That's over.

FRANKIE: Oh, yeah?

LUKE: Consider it sorted. You are now entering Luketown – population you.

FRANKIE: Do you always travel at this velocity?

LUKE: It's the only way to travel. Frankie… I've never done this before – I've only ever brought one woman here before you and that was years ago. I've never even been on a date before. I've been a butterfly collector. Caught a few – Phone-boxes – clubs – streets near train stations – Butterflies are everywhere. But Butterflies don't last. I'm looking for something less evanescent.

FRANKIE: Effervescent?

LUKE: Evanescent. Ephemeral. Fleeting. I'm looking for something incandescent – but with a life-span. I'm looking for a bird of paradise. I'm hoping that's you.

FRANKIE: You're looking for a wife off of your first date. That's optimistic.

LUKE: The day Mum and Dad met she didn't even fancy him. But he took one look and told her she was gonna marry him. They were together seventeen years. Sometimes you just know.

FRANKIE: You know I'm pre-op, don't you?

LUKE: I read your ad.

FRANKIE: The breasts are real – but I've still got…

She looks down at her lap.

LUKE: It's cool.

FRANKIE: It's shrunk a bit from the hormones – but it's still there.

LUKE: You wanna show me?

FRANKIE looks around.

Fuck them.

(Sliding down in his seat.) I'll show you mine.

FRANKIE: *(Laughing.)* Luke!

LUKE: Relax babe, it's only a Willie…

(Undoes his trousers.) See?

FRANKIE leans back and glances under the table.

He's a gentleman – knows to stand up upon meeting a lady. Frankie, meet Big Luke who lives downstairs. Big Luke – Frankie.

(Sitting up.) Now you.

FRANKIE looks at him for a moment – then slides down in her seat and lifts her skirt…

(Encouraging, curious, but not salacious.) Yeah… Yeah… Yeah.

(Sees it.) Cool.

(Picks up the menu.) Hungry?

FRANKIE: You okay?

LUKE: No. I need to take my mind off you for moment – otherwise I'll say something stupid.

He smiles. FRANKIE smiles back uncertainly.

Oh my life, check out that smile. Fuck it. I'll say it. You're gonna marry me.

FRANKIE: *(Laughs.)* What are you like?

LUKE: I'm a Prospect boy. We know what we want. I don't want just any girl you could find anywhere. I want a girl with something extra.

FRANKIE: Well, you found one of them.

LUKE: That's why I know you're gonna marry me.

FRANKIE: I wish I could.

LUKE: Wishes are for fishes, doll. Do it.

FRANKIE: Last time I checked it was still against the law?

LUKE: Well, let's change the law and check again. I like a mission.

LUKE's phone rings. LUKE answers it.

Don't go away, babe, yeah? Whaddup?

MARK: Bruv.

LUKE: Bruv.

MARK: Where the fuck, bruv?

LUKE: Been delayed, bruv.

MARK: Sort it out, bruv.

LUKE: There in five, bruv.

MARK: You know it.

LUKE: Believe.

LUKE hangs up – smiles ruefully at FRANKIE.

Sorry babe.

ONE YEAR AGO – MATTHEW & LUCY'S FLAT

LUCY: It's eighty-five degrees. The city is oozing around us – our bare legs are sticking to your leather car seats and we're purring and prowling through the streets with the roof down. We're feline. We're lupine.

MATTHEW: We're hungry…

LUCY: There's a boy on the side of the road, lean and leggy – like you must've been. He's kicking a ball off the wall, he's licking a lolly – his hair is shining with sweat. He looks up and sees us pulling over to the kerb. He recognizes you.

MATTHEW: He knows me.

LUCY: You're his idol – He trusts you. As he approaches, bouncing the football like a basketball, we can see he's like fourteen – thirteen –

MATTHEW: – Twelve.

LUCY: His lips are stained red. His skin is all covered in salty diamonds. He must smell so fresh…

MATTHEW: He smells so… Young…

LUCY: He's leaning into the car across you to talk to me… flirting with us… His body is so supple against you – intentionally off-balance – all you have to do is gently…put your foot down…

MATTHEW: …and he's our'n.

NOW – CAR

LUKE driving. He looks at FRANKIE – who looks at him.

LUKE: What?

FRANKIE: What?

LUKE: *(Laughs.)* What?

FRANKIE: Oh, it's okay for you to look at me…

LUKE: Look right back, it's cool.

FRANKIE: I'm just wondering what your mum is like. Is she strong like you?

LUKE: No, she's strong like you. You'll see. …When you meet her. …You will meet her. …You don't believe me. You think I'm all chat – you think I'm gonna put you in a box and pull you out and pump you up on Friday nights.

(Pause.) You wanna meet her?

FRANKIE: Who?

LUKE: Mama Luke. Bridie Prospect. My mum.

FRANKIE: What, now?

LUKE: All we have is now, babe.

FRANKIE: I don't think either of us are ready for that, Luke.

LUKE: I'm ready.

FRANKIE: I meant me and your mum.

(Thinks.) What about your brothers?

LUKE: Ask for yourself if you like.

He pulls over alongside MARK.

Alright, bruv?

MARK goes round to the passenger seat.

FRANKIE: Oh, Luke…

MARK: If you call being stood on the side of the road waiting for me own fucking motor to show up 'alright'.

MARK, about to open the passenger door, sees FRANKIE.

MARK: Sorry babe…   FRANKIE: Oh! Sorry…
Didn't see you…   I can get in the back…

MARK: Nah, nah, babe, you're alright…

MARK gets in the back, leans back in his seat and watches…taking FRANKIE in.

It's cool, yeah…

LUKE pulls out.

LUKE: Just giving Frankie a quick lift down Tooley Street.

MARK: That's nice.

LUKE: This is my brother, Mark…

MARK: 'right Frank?

FRANKIE: Nice to meet you. Heard a lot about you.

MARK: All bad, I hope.

LUKE: So – Matthew sorting things out with Lucy?

MARK: Matthew's running.

LUKE: S' he alright?

MARK: Fucked if I know. I mean, what the fuck do I know about anything, know what I mean? Is anyone alright? Are you alright?

LUKE: Me, bruv?

MARK: Yeah, you bruv.

LUKE: I'm sweet bruv.

MARK: Yeah. You're sweet. How 'bout you, Frankie? You sweet?

LUKE: Don't she look sweet, bruv?

MARK: Dunno bruv – can't really see from here. Didn't really get a good look – she sort of caught me on the hop. She smells sweet though, bruv.

(Inhales.) Angel – Thierry Mugler.

LUKE: Luke's got a stall down East Street on Sundays.

MARK: Designer only. No knock-offs.

FRANKIE: Down the Walworth Road end, cut-price Calvins and Clinique? I shop there every week! Are they your beautiful two kids?

MARK: They only look beautiful. Little fuckers.

LUKE: My niece and nephew, doll. See the resemblance?

FRANKIE: So, you're with Janine Lockwood?

MARK: She's my missus, yeah.

(Pause.) You know her?

FRANKIE: From St Hildegarde's. She was in my class.

MARK: Janine was in your class?

FRANKIE: Ohhh, yeah.

MARK: What was she like?

FRANKIE: Them days? Low-key.

MARK/LUKE: 'Low key?'

MARK: Janine? I think you've got her mixed up, mate.

LUKE: Babe.

MARK: Do what?

LUKE: She ain't a 'mate', bruv, she's a 'babe'.

MARK: Janine was low-key? Do us a favour.

FRANKIE: Well, you know that was before.

MARK: 'Before?'

FRANKIE: Before her mum went back to Jamaica with that guy she married.

MARK: You knew her mum?

FRANKIE: Well, I never knew her but I was there.

MARK: 'There'?

FRANKIE: You know – that day. I'm sorry – I shouldn't have said nothing.

LUKE steers to the kerb…

LUKE: Here you go…

MARK: What day?

LUKE gets out and goes round to the passenger seat.
What day?

LUKE opens the door…

FRANKIE: I'm sorry, Mark…

She starts to get out – MARK reaches out to grab her.

MARK: What fucking day?

LUKE: Bruv!

FRANKIE: Luke. It's not for me to tell you, Mark. I thought you knew.

MARK: How do you know I don't know? How do you know I'm not testing you?

MARK lets go…

FRANKIE: Well, everyone knows everything, really, don't they? But that don't mean they shouldn't ask.

MARK: I'm asking you.

FRANKIE: I'm not your missus, Mark I think you should talk to her.

MARK: You really haven't seen her in while, have you?

LUKE: Come on babe…

He helps her out of the car. Leans back in the car.

I'm gonna walk Frankie to her door, bruv – will you be alright on your own?

MARK: Fucked if I know.

(Before LUKE can move away.) Bruv…

LUKE: Bruv.

MARK: Is she what you really want?

LUKE: She's a dream come true, mate.

Pause.

MARK: She's alright. Go for it.

LUKE smiles.

You don't give a fuck if I think she's alright, anyway, do you?

LUKE: I do as it goes.

MARK: Sweet.

LUKE: Sweet.

MARK: Don't leave her stood on the street, mate – it's rough round here. Go on, fuck off!

LUKE: Laters.

LUKE leads FRANKIE away towards her door.

After a long moment, MARK climbs into the front seat and starts the engine…

FIVE YEARS AGO – MARK & JANINE'S LIVING ROOM

JANINE sleeps. MARK crawls over her – he rests his head on her stomach and listens… JANINE stirs…

JANINE: Lost something?

MARK: Just getting a sneak preview.

(He reacts.) Shit! *I* felt that one!

JANINE: Tell me about it – I swear, man, I'm a taxi for Tom and Jerry.

MARK: They having another ruck in there?

(To stomach.) Oy! You two break it up!

(Head to kicking stomach.) Ow! Cheeky bastards! Walking all over their poor old dad already… Hold up…

(Cod posh.) Would you two mind terribly being quiet? Your mother's trying to nap.

MARK listens, then smiles up at JANINE, who smiles back…

JANINE: Textbook dad.

MARK: To match a model mum.

(Kisses her.) See, I've been studying… My kids ain't having my dad…

JANINE: Or mine.

MARK: No spankings, no lying to 'em…

JANINE: Or making bullshit promises…

MARK: And we're never gonna say 'Cause I said so', instead of explaining. We're gonna be posh parents.

JANINE: So now we're gonna have them middle-class type kids – running all over the restaurant screaming out of control…

MARK: We'll be terrorized. God, ain't there a mum and dad school we can go to?

JANINE: Of course, in Jamaican families the mother is usually in charge of discipline.

MARK: Yeah? In Irish families the mother's in charge of the guilt.

JANINE: *(Hits him lightly.)* Don't make me laugh it makes my belly hurt! For serious, though – they reckon men get too carried away.

MARK: Some of us can't help ourselves…

JANINE: It's like – mum is closest – so punishment is in perspective – if you've got a distant dad, you know, out, like, working all day and it's all 'Wait 'til your father gets home' – and the kids are like crapping themselves and then he comes home and whips 'em and then that's all he is, you get me? But mum is always there – she's food and she's clean clothes and whatever – you know she loves you really, no matter what. What? What?

MARK: Why does dad have to be distant? That's such bollocks!

JANINE: You won't be distant, baby… And you won't be the punisher… Mama's here to take the brunt…

MARK: *(To stomach.)* Mama's here to take the brunt… so dad don't have to act the cunt. Oh my God…

(Curling up to her.) Janine, Janine, Janine… I really fucking love you…

JANINE: *(Kissing MARK.)* As wise as you are handsome…

MARK: *(Kissing JANINE.)* …And lucky.

NOW – FRANKIE'S DOOR STEP

LUKE and FRANKIE approach the front door.

FRANKIE: Is your brother alright?

LUKE: Well, he liked you, I reckon.

(Smiles.) Caught his eyes wandering.

FRANKIE: I shouldn't have said nothing. I thought he knew.

LUKE turns her to face him.

LUKE: Babe. You don't say sorry to me. Never. Your sorry days are over. 'Course you thought he knew. Man and wife should share everything. Tell me everything.

FRANKIE: About Janine?

LUKE: About you. Everything. You got any brothers?

FRANKIE: Four.

LUKE: Four? Show-off.

FRANKIE: You got two?

LUKE: Three. You lot close?

FRANKIE: Used to be.

FRANKIE thinks a while. LUKE reaches out and straightens a lock of her hair.

Well – good night.

She kisses him quickly on the cheek and turns away fumbling to put her key in the lock.

LUKE: So, is that it? You're gonna leave me on the doorstep all numb and dumb and overflowing with come?

FRANKIE: Luke. Are you a pirate?

LUKE: Come again?

FRANKIE: Some men, you know – they come up alongside… greeting you as fellow sailors. You allow them aboard and they rob you blind – then they're gone in search of new ships. There are thiefs who don't need to steal, they just need to know they can.

LUKE: I ain't a thief, Frankie. Not no more. Not from you. For you.

FRANKIE: You see – that's the problem – You always know what to say. They're the ones to watch out for.

LUKE: Okay. What do you want?

FRANKIE: I'm sorry, Luke, it's just…

LUKE: You want it in writing? Skywriting? Up in lights in Leicester Square?

FRANKIE: Luke…

LUKE: You want me to get a tattoo of your name?

(Pulling out a pen-knife.) I'll carve it in my arm right here, yeah?

FRANKIE: Luke.

LUKE: I ain't a playa, Frankie. I don't play.

(Taking her hand.) Come here…

He leads her with gentle firmness back towards the street…

Come on… Come on…

They're out on the street. We hear the passing traffic…

LUKE takes FRANKIE in his arms and kisses her.

The horn of a passing car – without breaking the kiss, LUKE gives them the finger.

Which side're your fucked-up neighbours?

FRANKIE: Neighbours?

LUKE: This side? That side? The one's what are giving you shit.

FRANKIE: Why?

LUKE picks a door and beats on it…

LUKE: He-LLO-OH!

FRANKIE: Luke!

…then crosses to the other door…

FRANKIE: Okay, you can come in! Luke!

LUKE: He-LLO-OH!

LUKE kicks and beats the door…

FRANKIE: LUKE!

The door opens.

LUKE: Alright, mate? I'm from next door.

NOW – OUTSIDE LUCY'S FLAT.

MARK: Lucy? Lucy, man, it's Mark. I just wanna have a quick word, yeah? I'm alone yeah? It ain't about Matt. It's about your sister. It's about Janine.

LUCY opens the door.

NOW – LUCY'S FLAT

LUCY talks to MARK.

LUCY: Mum reckoned we had it soft. Her mum used to whip her every morning in advance –

JANINE/LUCY: Crack!

LUCY: That's for all the things you're gonna do! That granny won't see!

JANINE: With licks you learn!

LUCY: What you can't hear, you can feel! Dad was raised different, soft-spoken and gentle – always smiling. It'd hurt your eyes, that smile – it was the sun. Seemed like every time he turned away everything withered. You know how mums shout, 'Wait til your father gets home'? Our Mum'd whisper…

JANINE: 'Wait 'til your father goes out'

LUCY: …and we'd start shaking right then.

JANINE and LUCY pace anxiously.

JANINE: Now look what you done, man…

LUCY: I never done nothing!

JANINE: Shh! She's gonna hear you!

LUCY: It weren't me – I never done nothing!

JANINE: Shut it! Bitch!

She punches LUCY in the arm.

LUCY: OW!

JANINE: Fuck's sake, man! Shh!

She puts her hand over LUCY's mouth…

Shhh, please, shush!

(Rocking her sister.) Shush! Shush, baby girl, shush… I'm sorry, Lucy-Lucy – I didn't mean it…

It's okay…

LUCY: *(Whispers.)* I hate Mum. Will I go to Hell?

JANINE: It's alright, Lucy-Lucy… I won't tell God…

We hear the front door closing. They tense up…

LUCY: And then that sound…the front door closing… We'd run to the window to look out at the eclipse – Daddy walking away – and as soon he reached the corner – we'd hear her footsteps on the stairs – thunder approaching…

(To JANINE.) She's coming!

JANINE: I know.

LUCY: *(Dashing about.)* We gotta hide!

JANINE: There's nowhere!

LUCY: Behind the curtains!

JANINE: There's nowhere!

LUCY: Climb out the window!

JANINE: There's nowhere.

The door opens. LUCY runs behind JANINE and collapses…

LUCY: Mummmeeeeee! Please!

I always wondered if Dad knew. But how could he? He wouldn't have let us live that way. Daddy was the good guy. But you never asked about all this. You asked about 'That day'. That was the day Nelson Mandela was freed. Miracle day. Our teachers wanted every class to stay and watch it live on TV. Don't know why we even tried asking. Mum was gonna say no. But that day when three-thirty came – Janine met me in the empty school yard and she led me back inside, as if to say…

JANINE: Some punishments are worth taking.

LUCY: Now we're in the school hall watching the Walk to Freedom. And we feel something at the door…and look round…and there she is, staring in through the glass and it's the end of the world. But Janine turns to me…

JANINE: 'It's okay'.

LUCY: And my little sister gets up and steps out into the hallway. I know I should have been stronger. I should have been braver. I was the oldest. But I turned back to Nelson's walk and wished myself a life way, walking free in South Africa. Until Mum screamed.

(Turning her head.) Mum screamed. Our mother was on her knees. At my sister's feet. A slash cross her cheek and her

eyes unbelieving. As the teacher gently took the broken pencil from Janine's soft fist. I saw liberation fly away. I pictured us imprisoned – incarcerated – in care. But Teacher never told. Mum never told. She never spoke round us ever again. Until the day she dropped us off with our nan and flew away with no goodbye – and me and Janine – Five and six – for the first time we were free and Janine swore she would never be afraid again.

Pause.

MARK: Fuck. Why didn't I know none of this?

(Thinks.) What do you think your dad should've done?

LUCY: I used to think I knew what people should do. But I don't. I used to wish he'd tried to love her less. But how do you love someone less?

ONE YEAR AGO – MATTHEW & LUCY'S FLAT

MATTHEW is pacing up and down, drinking. LUCY hurries in.

LUCY: He's out.

MATTHEW: He's out?

LUCY sits down and cuts up a line…

LUCY: Like a light. Out.

MATTHEW: Fuck!

LUCY: And he's smiling.

MATTHEW: Smiling?

LUCY snorts a line.

LUCY: Beaming.

MATTHEW: Fuck – I wish I could have a line. I need to get more fucked-up.

LUCY: You can.

MATTHEW: You know I can't.

LUCY: When was the last time they tested you?

MATTHEW: Month ago.

LUCY: Before that?

MATTHEW: Seven – eight months…

LUCY: Well then.

MATTHEW: It's random testing, not regular.

LUCY: So you get suspended. They never fucking let you play anyway – It's been a year at least. Well, fuck 'em, give yourself a treat.

MATTHEW: Fuck 'em.

(Snorts a line, shakes his head horse-like.) Shit! Yes! He looks younger than he said.

LUCY: He's lying because he wants to be old enough for what's gonna happen.

MATTHEW: What's gonna happen?

LUCY: What you both want to happen. What we both want to happen. For us to have secrets that no one else shares – for us to be bound together forever. Like your brothers and you – and my sister and me.

MATTHEW: Like family.

LUCY: Now you know how much I love you. How I will do anything for you.

(Sniffs another line.) I will kill for you – I will give birth for you –

MATTHEW snorts…

…anything that satisfies that craving I know you feel…

MATTHEW: You'll give birth?

LUCY: I will breed lovers for you.

Silence. They hear something in the next room. Tension.

MATTHEW: What's he doing?

They listen.

LUCY: He's crying… Maybe it's a nightmare. I swear he was smiling.

MATTHEW: Just open the front door and let him leave…

LUCY snorts a third line and leaves…MATTHEW stares into space listening intently. After a while LUCY returns, she closes the door behind her and leans against it. MATTHEW doesn't look at her.

LUCY: He won't go.

MATTHEW: Wake him up.

LUCY: He says he's awake. He says he won't go 'til he's spoken to you.

MATTHEW: I can't be trusted.

LUCY: And he won't stop crying. Can you hear him?

MATTHEW: Tell him to stop!

LUCY: He won't stop!

MATTHEW: Tell him to go!

LUCY: He won't go! You tell him!

MATTHEW: Go home!

LUCY: He won't go!

MATTHEW: Go home!

LUCY: He won't go!

MATTHEW runs out of the room

MATTHEW: Go hooooooooome!

MARK & JANINE'S FLAT

MARK arrives, with a rose, bouncing keys in his hand.

MARK: Daddy's home!

(Pause.) Hello?

JANINE comes in.

JANINE: Keep it down, yeah, babe? I just got 'em down for the night.

(Kisses him.) 'right, gangsta?

MARK: *(Giving her the rose.)* 'Right, gangsta bitch? They been giving you grief, is it?

JANINE: They just been kids, you know, whatever. I've got 'em under control.

MARK: Got 'em under manners yeah? I'll just go up and give 'em a kiss.

JANINE: Markman! *(Pulling him back to her…)*

If they see daddy they'll want to get up again…

(Kisses him.) You'll just upset 'em…

MARK: Okay…

(Kiss.) I swear…

(Kiss.) I'll just peek in for a nano, yeah?

JANINE: That's right – do what you always do. Show me up. And who is it who has to deal with 'em in the morning, when they're all tired and grumpy and they have to be got off to school? Who has to be the bad guy?

MARK watches as she paces about tidying things up.

MARK: I just want to tuck 'em in… But it's cool.

(Summoning the strength to ask.) Are they alright, Janine?

JANINE looks at him.

JANINE: Well, what you waiting for? Go and check. Go on. Go!

MARK: It's cool. I'll let 'em sleep.

(Pause.) What's for dinner?

JANINE: No, come on – I'll go with you. Let's do an inventory

(Hitting him with the rose.) – two kids – four legs, four arms – no bruises no bleeding…

MARK: …Neen, Neen, I'm sorry, yeah? I just…	JANINE: …Twenty needy little fingers – two greedy screaming little mouths!

They hear something…

Now look. Thanks a lot yeah?

She goes into the kid's bedroom. And through the baby monitor we hear…

(JANINE offstage.) What you doing awake? What did I tell you? What – did – I – tell – you? WHAT DID I TELL YOU? WHAT DID I FUCKING TELL YOU!!

As she screams and slaps… MARK listens – marooned.

ONE YEAR AGO – THE OTHER ROOM

The room is dark. MATTHEW comes running in. He stops.

MATTHEW: Are you there, mate?

BOY: I'm over here.

MATTHEW tries to find him in the dark.

MATTHEW: Sorry, man, you gotta go now.

BOY: No, thank you.

MATTHEW: What do you mean, no thank you? You've gotta go.

BOY: Why?

MATTHEW: Because you shouldn't be here. Because it ain't safe.

BOY: What if I don't wanna be safe?

MATTHEW: It ain't up to you.

BOY: I know what you wanna do. It's alright. I'm used to it. I meet people all the time.

MATTHEW: You meet people?

BOY: They do things to me.

MATTHEW: What things?

BOY: Anything. Everything. It's alright. I don't mind. I'm experienced.

MATTHEW: How old are you?

BOY: How old do you want me to be? It's alright, mister – I don't want money.

MATTHEW: Money?

BOY: Some give me money. I just wanna sleep.

MATTHEW: You can't sleep here, I'm sorry.

BOY: If you just touch me for a bit, I can go home and I can sleep. I've got tablets but they don't work.

MATTHEW: You really got to go now, okay?

BOY: I'm too tired to go. I'm too tired to move. If you just touch me I can sleep. It's the only thing that works. Go on, mate…

MATTHEW: How long have you been doing this?

BOY: Since I remember. I know I'm not right. I know I'm sick. I know I'm dirty. What do you do when what you are is so dirty no one wants to touch you?

MATTHEW: I do want to touch you – I just…can't.

BOY: I understand. I'm dirty.

MATTHEW: It ain't you that's dirty.

BOY: You won't touch me.

MATTHEW: Because it's wrong.

BOY: What do you do when everything you are is wrong?

MATTHEW: I don't know.

BOY: I do.

> *He reaches out, takes MATTHEW's hand and draws it towards him.*

NOW – PARIS & PERSEPHONE'S BEDROOM

MARK peeks round the door. He whispers.

MARK: You alright? You lot…! What you doing up? Your mum'll go…

> *(Eyes adjusting in the dark.)* Seph? What you doing standing there, Princess? Where's your nightie? Seph? Seph?

He comes forward – tries to pick her up.

Shit!

He has stood in something wet.

Okay… Okay…

Carefully he picks her up.

I've got you – it's okay…

Holding his daughter in his arms, he wriggles his shoes loose on his feet.

I know what Mummy said, Princess – but Mummy sent me up to say you can move now. She said the game's over and you can move…

He takes a long step out of the shoes, avoiding the puddle surrounding. He puts her down on the floor.

There you go… Game's over, yeah? And guess who's the winner?

He picks up an item of clothing off the floor and starts to wipe her down…

Miss Persephone Prospect. The winner!

(Looking around.) Where's your brother?

MARK lies on the floor…to peer under the bed…

Hey… You alright, little Geezer?

He crawls across…

Try and not cry, Seph, you're scaring your brother. Par! It's only me, man… It's only Daddy…

He reaches under the bed straining…

Par! I got you! Daddy's got you!

(He gets bitten.) Ow! Fuck!

(Reaching again.) Par! Don't crawl away from me, mate. It's dirty under there. There might be spiders, man. Or rats. Come on, man! Come on, Geezer. Please? Please Paris…

(Starts to cry.) Come on Geeze. Please, I'll be your best friend…don't cry, yeah?

MARK starts to cry and cry, overwhelmed…

Please don't cry…

MARK lies there… Crying.

ONE YEAR AGO – MATTHEW & LUCY'S PLACE

LUCY is snorting coke. MATTHEW comes in, drawn and tired. He kneels beside her and snorts. They do not look at one another.

LUCY: Has he gone?

MATTHEW nods – he starts to cry – then sob – then weeps uncontrollably.

NOW – FRANKIE'S FLAT

LUKE, bare torso covered in blood – sits happily drinking a glass of milk. FRANKIE puts antiseptic on his knuckles.

LUKE: I like your place, babe.

(Grins at her.) You got taste.

(Looking around.) Something missing, though…don't you reckon, Frankie? A man, maybe?

FRANKIE: I reckon you're mental.

LUKE: You let me in, though, dincha?

FRANKIE: Oh, my God, look at all this blood.

LUKE: *(Shrugs.)* 'Ain't my blood.

> *FRANKIE puts down the cotton wool.*

Hey, don't stop, babe. I like it when you pamper me.

FRANKIE: You can't stay.

LUKE: What? You want me to sort out the neighbours on the other side n'all? You drive a hard bargain, woman.

FRANKIE: I know I'm supposed to be grateful. I'm supposed to snatch the chance to be a Geezer's Bird in trembly lucky hands. I used to be that kind of girl once. But I was almost your type of bloke before that and I know how scared you really are and I know this ain't real. Handsome men don't just swoop down out of nowhere to slay dragons and sweep girls off their feet and fall in love at first sight and they all live happily ever after. They don't.

LUKE: Yeah, and frogs don't just turn back into the beautiful princesses they were all along. Fairytales don't just happen, babe. You make 'em happen.

FRANKIE: This ain't a fairytale, Luke. This is real. My neighbours are real. This blood is real. South London is real. I'm real. And you're dreaming.

LUKE: Yeah... Brilliant ain't it?

> *LUKE coughs – milk and blood spatters FRANKIE's stunned face.*

Shit.

(Wiping weakly at her face.) Sorry babe.

> *LUKE passes out.*

ONE YEAR AGO – MATTHEW AND LUCY'S PLACE

MATTHEW sits crying uncontrollably, he holds the phone in his hand. LUCY watching him, wild-eyed and fucked up. JOHN is beating on the door.

JOHN: MATTHEW, MAN! MATTMAN!

> *JOHN charges the door. It bursts open and he sees MATTHEW.*

Fucking hell, bruv.

NOW – STREET

MATTHEW running.

NOW – HOTEL ROOM/BRIDIE'S FLAT

MARK on the phone. BRIDIE sits up with a smoke.

MARK: Did I wake you up, Mum?

BRIDIE: You're alright, son…

MARK: Has Janine rung?

> *BRIDIE looks across at JANINE – who stands watching.*

BRIDIE: Should she have? She walked out on you? You two had a barney?

MARK: Not exactly. I've got the kids with me, Mum.

BRIDIE: The kids?

MARK: They're asleep. I took 'em down the hospital.

BRIDIE: Hospital?

MARK: Mum, it ain't her fault – she's under pressure – misses work – misses freedom. She's frustrated.

BRIDIE: Who is?

MARK: Janine. She gets carried away – like Dad used to. You know – Don't know her own strength. It's no big thing – but the kids are scared, Mum, I can't take 'em home yet. I gotta put a smile on their face. It's gonna be fine.

BRIDIE: You can bring 'em here the night if you like.

MARK: She'll come there, mum – I'm surprised she ain't there already. They're shit-scared of her. I gotta make 'em alright first.

> *BRIDIE beckons JANINE over to listen.*

BRIDIE: So, where you taken 'em?

MARK: We're at the Marriott. It's got a pool. I'm gonna take 'em on the Eye tomorrow. I've been promising 'em from time. When she calls there just tell her we're alright and I'll call her tomorrow.

> *JANINE leaves.*

BRIDIE: Why don't you call her?

MARK: I don't know what to say. You know what I mean, Mum… Back in the day…when it was Dad… I used to blame you. Now I am you.

So busy trying not to be him. I turned into you.

(Pause.) …Mum? I love you Mum.

(Pause.) Alright, Mum, I'll call you later.

BRIDIE: Alright, son.

She hangs up.

NOW – SUNAI'S FLAT

SUNAI arrives to find JOHN waiting, holding a rose.

JOHN: You ain't changed the locks.

SUNAI: I know.

JOHN: Where you been?

SUNAI: Walking. Where've you been?

She sits down. She slips off her coat. They sit.

JOHN: So you're just not gonna tell me.

(Pause.) You're not gonna tell me. About the baby. You gonna get rid of it? You gonna be a single mother? You got a plan that don't include me.

SUNAI: You know all my plans include you. Mad as I am.

JOHN: Let's start again. My mum reckons you're pregnant.

SUNAI: And if I am?

JOHN: I'll marry you.

SUNAI: Me? The white man's concubine? You would lower yourself so far?

JOHN: My baby won't be born a bastard.

SUNAI: Bastards aren't born, Johnny – they're made.

JOHN: Fucking hell, Sunai, don't fucking put me through it – I know I fucking deserve it. But I can't take it. Just marry me.

SUNAI: Even if I ain't pregnant?

JOHN: Well, are you?

SUNAI: Will you marry me if I ain't?

JOHN: *(Jumping up.)* Sunai!

> *(He paces.)* What do you *want?* What are you hanging about for the entire fucking time? Why ain't you changed the locks? What are you waiting for?

SUNAI: Not this.

JOHN: Well, fucking hell, Sunai, this is the best I fucking got.

SUNAI: I don't want nothing you're not prepared to give. If it's dragged out of you I don't want it.

JOHN: Well, give me a fucking clue, girl. I'm fucking stranded here.

> *(Backing away slowly toward the door.)* I shouldn't have come here, man – the water's fucking rising round me. Look at you – you don't even know you're doing it, do you?

SUNAI: Doing what?

JOHN: Being beautiful. You're deadly, you are. Beautiful and fucking deadly. Can't you just stop it?

> *(Hits the rose against her chair.)* Fucking stop it! Stop it! STOP IT!

> *The rose is destroyed, so is JOHN.*

> Why can't you have some mercy woman? Why can't you stop?

> I'm no fucking good for no one Sunai. I'm fucked. I'm a cunt.

SUNAI: I know.

JOHN: I'm a nasty bitter twisted little prick.

SUNAI: I know.

JOHN: Our children wouldn't be safe with me.

SUNAI: I know. I shouldn't love you. I've tried. I've read the Koran over and over – but there's nothing for this.

JOHN: Let's read it together.

> *JOHN sees something on his hands.*

> Sunai!

SUNAI: What?

> *The palms of JOHN's hands are bloody.*

JOHN: Sunai! I'm bleeding! I'm bleeding!

SUNAI: Johnny?

JOHN: I'm bleeding! I'm bleeding! I'm bloody crucified! It's all the sins, Sunai! It's all the sins and the evil! They've crucified me!

SUNAI: Johnny, calm down! Johnny Johnny!

SUNAI gets a hold of him…

Johnny! Shush!

He stares at her, wild-eyed.

Johnny, it's okay…it's just the thorns from the rose, Johnny.

She dabs at his wounds…

JOHN: The thorns?

SUNAI: See? Just the thorns from the rose…

JOHN: The thorns…from the rose.

NOW – HOTEL ROOM

JANINE is outside, knocking on the door.

JANINE: Mark!

MARK approaches the door. He listens.

Mark! It's me! Mark? If you want me to go away I'll go. Just say. Do you want me to go?

MARK opens the door. JANINE is standing there.

Can I come in?

MARK stands aside. JANINE steps in. She hands him something that looks like a credit card.

MARK: What's 'at?

JANINE: The key.

MARK: They give you a key?

JANINE: I'm your wife.

MARK: Why'd you knock?

JANINE: I wanted you to let me in. They sleeping?

MARK: Yeah.

JANINE: So – Are we over?

MARK: We just needed to get away for a night.

JANINE: From me?

MARK: Janine…

JANINE: Is that what they told you? That they needed to get away from me? Did they say that? Did you ask them?

MARK: They're fucking terrified, babe…

JANINE: You didn't need to, did you?

(Beat.) I got it wrong, didn't I? I swear I don't know how anyone gets it right. It's like remember what you told me? About how your dad used to punish your brother? And how a part of you wondered why he never hurt you like that? Because…

MARK: …at least he touched him.

JANINE: That's what I'm trying to do. Touch them.

(Pause.) I don't know how to touch my own kids. I look at you with them two – how you light each other up and I'm a foreigner. These are all just excuses. I don't have a clue. So, now it's down to you. Whatever you say goes. I want to change. I don't want to feel like this. I don't want to be this lonely. I'll do whatever you say. Because only you can save me. Do you want me to go, Mark?

MARK: *(Shakes his head, barely able to talk.)* No.

JANINE: Do you want me to stay?

MARK: Yes.

JANINE moves towards him.

JANINE: Can I touch you?

MARK: Yes.

JANINE puts her arms around MARK.

JANINE: …Thank you.

MARK puts his arms round JANINE. MARK's phone starts to ring. They look at it together.

NOW – BRIDIE'S FLAT

BRIDIE sits smoking. MATTHEW arrives. He's been running.

MATTHEW: Mum? What you doing sitting up?

   He sits beside her. Looks around…

BRIDIE: Wondering what happened to our party.

MATTHEW: Sorry, Mum. Did Dad ever say sorry?

   Silence. MATTHEW's phone starts to ring. BRIDIE exhales…

BRIDIE: Sorry ain't all it's cracked up to be, love.

   Pause.

MATTHEW: Well…

BRIDIE: Phone.

NOW – HOSPITAL

JOHN performing press-ups – MARK on his mobile.

MARK: Fucking ansaphone! Luke, bruv, they won't let us in to see you or tell us what the fuck or nothing so if you're alive, get back, yeah, Mum's going spare.

JOHN: So he get in a ruck or what?

MARK: I dunno do I? Someone belled me that he was down casualty and then I called you lot.

BRIDIE: What'you mean 'someone'?

MARK: You'll see.

JOHN: Don't tell us that cunt's actually got a girlfriend?

MARK: You'll see.

BRIDIE: Fuck's sake, do you have to make a fucking Twilight Zone out of it?

   LUKE enters in his blood-soaked shirt. With FRANKIE.

LUKE: Alright, you wankers?

BRIDIE: Oh, my bleeding life!

MATTHEW: You alright, bruv?

MARK/JOHN: Shit!

FRANKIE: It's not as bad as it looks…

   EVERYONE looks at FRANKIE.

MARK: Been out biting necks or what, man?

LUKE: Slaying dragons, mate. Don't worry Mum, ain't my blood.

BRIDIE: So, what you doing in here, then?

FRANKIE: He fainted.

LUKE: Passed out, babe.

(Shrugs to his family.) Passed out didn't I?

BRIDIE: What the fuck you faint for?

LUKE: Maybe I can't stand the sight of blood.

FRANKIE: The doctor says Luke might be allergic to milk.

BRIDIE: Oh, you silly little git. What you drinking milk for?

FRANKIE: It was all I had in.

LUKE: It was all she had in.

FRANKIE: Sorry.

BRIDIE: Ain't your fault he ain't got the sense he was born with, sweetheart. Milk. Fuck's sake. 'You ever gonna introduce us? 'scuse him, ain't his fault he was badly brought up.

LUKE: Mark, you've met – Johnboy – Matthew – Sunai – John's bird and Bridie – my mum.

(Taking FRANKIE's hand.) My girl – Frankie. She's been having trouble with some noisy neighbours. I had to go round and quiet 'em down a bit. No one disrespects a Prospect girl, you know what I'm saying?

FRANKIE: You all look like him.

MARK: Fuck, you really know how to cheer us up, mate.

(Catching LUKE's eye.) …Babe.

BRIDIE: Nice meeting you, Frankie.

MATTHEW: Nice to meet you, Frankie.

MARK: Alright, Frankie?

SUNAI: Hello, Frankie

LUKE: *(To JOHN.)* Johnboy? Johnboy?

JOHN: So, that's it then? Frankie's just one of the family now?

MARK: Leave it, bruv.

JOHN: And we're all blind again are we? Adam ain't got an apple. Just like Matthew ain't a burn-out…

MARK: Bruv, leave it.

JOHN: …Mark ain't a door-mat and I ain't a fucking loser. Why don't someone tell the real truth for once?

(To FRANKIE.) You know the truth, doncha, Frank? You know what she's screaming inside, doncha, mate?

MARK: Don't call her mate, bruv.

JOHN: Sorry, 'babe', is it?

LUKE: How 'bout you just don't call her nothing, yeah?

FRANKIE: It's okay, Luke.

JOHN: Save the forgiveness for Mum, Frank. She's the one what's thinking 'Queer.' But that's okay. Another son, another let-down – now she's got a full set of fuck-ups. Burnout – doormat – loser – queer.

BRIDIE: John, your brother asked you to leave it.

JOHN: You leave it. You fucking leave it! I fucked-up seven years back and you ain't never let me forget it.

BRIDIE: You've never let me let you forget it! Limping about like a fucking kicked dog the whole time. Don't you get bored of feeling sorry for yourself? It weren't my fault you were on the rob and it ain't my fault you got caught.

JOHN: Only I never got caught did I? I gived myself up – 'cause your precious first-born told me to. Yeah, the golden boy burnout who gets the party for coming out of the fucking nuthouse 'You're aw minor, bruv – trust me, Bruv' Bish-bosh – cut to banged-up muggins crying for his mum who's too busy feeling embarrassed to give a fuck. Not shame – that requires dignity that does – just good old-fashioned embarrassment – 'what will they say down the pub? My perfect little Cosa Nostra family's been shown up by my stupid little last-born. John the Loser, John the Lost.'

SUNAI: Johnny…

JOHN: You can shut up an' all! You're as bad as she is! – distracting me – confusing me! They say that truth hurts, darlin' – well, this is gonna be a fucking blood-bath! If you can't hack it, get out now, while you can.

BRIDIE: Mark, what's that word you call John?

MARK: Drama queen.

BRIDIE: Is this the best you do, drama queen? Call this a bloodbath? I've had three forceps deliveries and a baby born premature on the kitchen floor – this ain't a bloodbath – this is a fucking piece of piss. Do you really think I don't know none of this? When you gonna get it through your head that I know everything? Before it even happens, I know everything.

JOHN: 'Course! Mum knows everything!

BRIDIE: I know that if you'd told your brothers you'd been nicked twice before and if I hadn't've stupidly helped you keep it secret – they wouldn't've sacrificed you and you wouldn't've had your three strikes and you wouldn't've gone down for a silly little bit of fun and you wouldn't've broken my fucking heart. When you look in your child's face and you can see he's been fucked up the arse and he's pissed the bed and he's taking smack and he's scared shitless – You ain't embarrassed. You're fucking heartbroken.

JOHN: If you know everything before it happens, why'd I go down, then? Why didn't you step in and save me?

BRIDIE: 'Cause you couldn't be saved. You were that kind of kid. It was better you done three months then than thirty years later on. And you would have done. It was inevitable.

Pause.

JOHN: 'Inevitable'?

LUKE: She means it was your fate, bruv.

JOHN: I know what she fucking means, bruv!

MATTHEW: Bollocks.

BRIDIE: Do what?

MATTHEW: That's bollocks. Mum. You're talking bollocks. Fate is bollocks. Inevitathingy don't exist. We didn't have to sacrifice our brother – you didn't have to pretend you didn't know what Dad was doing to us. You let us down

Mum. I let these lot down. Family should protect each other not fuck each other.

BRIDIE: Don't waste time blaming your dad. He weren't the Axis of Evil. He was just sad and sick. You fucked yourselfs, darling. You can't protect someone from themself.

MARK: How would you know, Mum? You never tried.

BRIDIE: Oh, yeah, you bleedin' start! How'd he fuck *you* up? He never fucking laid a hand on you.

MARK: No Mum, he just blanked me. I'm a fucking black lesbian, Mum.

BRIDIE: Do what?

MARK: My skin fucking chafes me, my dick don't fit me – None of it fucking fits me, Mum. I just wanna jump right out of this stinking body and fucking run.

BRIDIE: And what about you, Luke? Am I to blame for you?

(Looking at FRANKIE.) Is this your revenge?

LUKE: No Mum, this is me. I just don't wanna feel so fucked-up no more. I wanna feel normal.

BRIDIE: Oh sweetheart. Ain't I taught you fuck all? This is normal. Do you think this is the life I lay on my teenage bed dreaming of? Dear Baby Jesus, please let me grow up and marry a fucking nonce? Let my kids be a gang of vicious bastards that every fucker fears and no fucker likes? Let me be an hard-face cow whose own family cringes when I touch 'em? Do you think your dad wanted to be evil? Do you think that there's anybody on this filthy planet what don't wake up hating their stinking decaying body and their under-educated lazy brain wondering how they turned into this pointless pile of lonely shit? I fucking read *books* when I was a little girl. I drank the fucking library *dry* – I was gonna go to galleries one day – my kids were gonna be Kennedies. Not Krays. Not cunts. But we know what I've got. And am I stood around crying about it? No. I'm getting on with it. Like I had to get on with it after I realized my dad was evil and my mum was weak. Like we'll all have to get on with it after we've finished this so-called conversation and you lot realize you have to face the fact that every sod has to face eventually – that the wind changed years ago and you're stuck as who you are whether you like it or not.

FRANKIE: Bollocks.

BRIDIE: What, you an' all? Who kicked your bleeding hutch?

FRANKIE: We ain't stuck, Bridie. We can make changes. We can shift. You can become more of what you feel and less of what you been made. We can grow into ourselves. We can become ourselves.

BRIDIE: Can we indeed. Anyone else want to put their oar in? Sunai?

SUNAI: She's right, Bridie.

BRIDIE: Of course she's right. Everyone's right and Mum's wrong.

SUNAI: Don't you want to be wrong, sometimes, Bridie? Don't you want more for your grand-kids? I do. I don't want my son to be afraid of love – my daughter to wait forever for her man to lose his fear. I want more. Bridie – I want love for my kids. And if all it takes is to be wrong. Then let me be wrong. You were wrong about John – he hasn't gone to prison for thirty years.

BRIDIE: Yet.

FRANKIE: Well, it ain't inevitable if it ain't happened yet, is it?

BRIDIE: That's the thing love. It has happened. Everything's happened before. And everything will happen again.

MATTHEW: And that's wrong. It's all wrong…

MATTHEW turns to his brothers.

…And I'm sorry.

He approaches his brothers one by one…

…I'm sorry bruv, I'm sorry bruv, I'm sorry bruv.

He turns to BRIDIE.

BRIDIE: Don't say it…

MATTHEW: I'm sorry Mum…

BRIDIE: Please Matthew…

Weakly resisting him, BRIDIE crumbles towards the ground, MATTHEW catches her, arms around her, rocking.

MATTHEW: I'm sorry Mum – I'm sorry Mum… I'm sorry I'm sorry I'm sorry…

BRIDIE: Matthew… Please…

After a long moment, BRIDIE gently steps away.

I know, son.

BRIDIE sits for a moment. Then looks round at her family.

What you lot looking at?

(To FRANKIE.) Oy – troublemaker – what's your name again, darlin'?

FRANKIE: Frankie.

BRIDIE: Come here, Frankie. Let's see you.

FRANKIE approaches BRIDIE, who looks her in the face.

Hands.

FRANKIE presents her hands. BRIDIE holds them – checking the feel of them.

You lot dun'narf get the pretty ones duncha? Don't know how you brood of ugly bastards do it.

(To FRANKIE.) And you don't know what you're getting yourself into, becoming a Prospect girl.

FRANKIE: Maybe I do.

BRIDIE: Well, then you're the first, love. The day I met their dad and he told me I was gonna marry him, there was no way – Too much like my dad – and I weren't gonna be like my mum. I was gonna get up out of their wreckage and walk away. And I told him that. And you know what he said? 'I understand'. And I was fucked. How could I leave the only one what understood me behind? Was we 'soul-mates'? 'Kindred spirits'? Any of that bollocks? Fucked if I knew – but someone understood me. So I married him. We went to our wedding on the 53 bus – halfway there I remembered we didn't have no cutlery in our bed-sit. So we jumped off and run in Woolworths, bought two knives, two forks, two plates, two bowls, two cups and the one spoon they had left, jumped back on the bus and went and got married. Afterwards, on the way to the pub I bought us a cake from Marks and I hid it from everyone at the reception 'til we got home and we could split it between the two of us. We shared our spoon and he lit a candle. To glimpse a future in someone's face is a fantastic thing. Then he went back out to celebrate with his mates and he never come home 'til the next morning. And we both knew. The future was over. Fate was bigger than us. It's none of it new, I know. It was all so bloody obvious. But that's the thing, ain't it – Everything's inevitable because nothing's original. We marry our parents and then we try and fix what they fucked up, because we're young and we're stupid and arrogant and we think our vow to not be our parents is not the same old vow they made and does not make us all the more like them. And there we are and we're our mother. Afraid to be without a husband so pretending to be a wife. Afraid to be a mother so pretending to be blind. Afraid to bleed so refusing to feel. And this is our normal. What I've done and what you'll do. Swearing to yourself you won't? Of course you are. See, I've been your age. All your ages and fuck knows enough ages since and the one thing I've learned is nobody knows how young they are. Well, maybe you've still got time – to choose the girl with a future in her face what sees a future in yours and save each other and protect your children and fix what your old man and mum fucked up. But you probably won't. And so we go on. The Fucked-up Prospects, hard-faced and hated, like their fore-fathers before 'em. Vile. Cursed. Damned. 'Time is it?

LUKE: 's almost light.

BRIDIE: Then it's nearly early. Well – let's get on with it. Let's go home and I'll make you lot breakfast, yeah? You got your motor, Sunai?

SUNAI: In the carpark.

BRIDIE: Bring it round the front, willya – you can take John, me, Luke and Frankie, yeah? Mark, you take Matthew and pick up Janine and the kids.

MARK nods…pulling out his phone. SUNAI leaves.

JOHN: I'll come with you, babe…

BRIDIE: Do you wanna call Lucy?

MATTHEW: I can't Mum. Lucy can't make it.

BRIDIE: That's a shame. Someone will, son.

MATTHEW: I dunno Mum.

BRIDIE: I do.

She puts her arm through his and they start to leave.

MARK: *(On phone.)* Alright, gangsta bitch?

LUKE: What about you, Mum?

BRIDIE: Oh, I'm past saving, me.

LUKE: Bollocks.

BRIDIE: Now, is that any way to talk to your mother?

LUKE: You know your trouble, duncha? You don't know how young you are.

BRIDIE: *(Smiles.)* You're a funny bugger.

(To FRANKIE.) He's a funny bugger.

(As they leave.) …Takes after me…

They leave.

Blackout.

End.

Rikki Beadle-Blair

Born and raised by his lesbian mother in South East London, Rikki learned to read at the age of three and wrote his first play aged seven, moving on to direction at the age of eleven. He attended the experimental Bermondsey Lampost Free School, where he could study any subject he liked and focused on theatre and film making.

Named several years running on the *Independent on Sunday*'s Pink List as one the 100 most influential gay people in Britain, Rikki has a life-long commitment to creating challenging, transformative entertainment in the mediums of Film, Theatre, Music, Television, Radio, Dance and Design. He created the production company Team Angelica to pursue these goals and share opportunities with performers, artists and practitioners from the widest possible range of backgrounds.

Rikki wrote *Stonewall* for BBC Films. Directed by Nigel Finch, *Stonewall* went on to win the audience awards at the London Film Festival and the San Francisco Lesbian and Gay film festival as well an award for Rikki at Outfest LA for Outstanding Screenwriting.

Among other television projects, Rikki wrote, directed and featured in the internationally successful Channel 4 series *Metrosexuality*, also composing the soundtrack.

His radio documentary, *The Roots of Homophobia* was awarded the Sony award for Best Documentary Feature.

He was a writer and the executive story editor for the US TV series, *Noah's Arc*, and was supervising director of debut films with first-time gay filmmakers as a director for the Out in Africa organization in South Africa.

Recently Rikki directed the short film *Souljah* by John Gordon, about a transgendered former child soldier, which won best film at the Rushes London Short film festival.

Rikki works extensively in theatre – creating 18 new plays in the last six years, including *twothousandandSex*, the stage version of *Stonewall* and for Theatre Royal Stratford East *Bashment*, *Familyman* and *Shalom Baby*, and directing new writing including

Stripped by Hannah Chalmers, *Step* by Lynette Lynton for the TRSE's Young Actor's Company and the upcoming *Slap* by Alexis Gregory.

In the last three years, Rikki has directed three successful feature films for his company Team Angelica: *Fit* about teenage sexuality and homophobic bullying which was distributed to every school in the UK and has become a phenomenon with screenings world-wide, *KickOff*, a comedy about a football match between a gay and straight football team and the film version of *Bashment* set in the word of homophobic hip-hop/ragga music; He has already made several more short films, including *Gently*, *7 Dials*, *Thrive*, *Alive*, and *Butterfly* commissioned by the Royal Albert Hall.

Rikki is currently working on his next films *FREE* which is the sequel to *FIT* plus *Lena*, an American play about Lena Horne, plus *Zebra*, a play for Che Walker.

Rikki is also a committed mentor, regularly teaching his In the Room career alignment course and one-on-one Career Clinic.

His self-help books *What I Learned Today* and *Reasons To Live* are available now through Team Angelica Books on www.teamangelica.com

OTHER RIKKI BEADLE-BLAIR TITLES

Shalom Baby
9781849432139

Bashment
9781840025828

Fit
9781849430807

Familyman
9781840028584

WWW.OBERONBOOKS.COM

Follow us on www.twitter.com/@oberonbooks
& www.facebook.com/oberonbook